K130

LIVIN

Abraham's

LIVING BY FAITH

Abraham's Example For Today

David Prior

HODDER AND STOUGHTON
LONDON SYDNEY AUCKLAND TORONTO

British Library Cataloguing in Publication Data

Prior, David
   Living by faith: Abraham's example for
   today. —— (Hodder Christian paperbacks)
   1. Abraham   2. Faith —— Case studies
   I. Title
   248.4   BA580.A3

   ISBN 0-340-39914-7

*Hodder and Stoughton Editorial Office: 47 Bedford Square, London
WC1B 3DP*

To my mother and father,

who first pointed the way,

with much love and increasing gratitude

CONTENTS

	Acknowledgements	8
	Introduction	9
1	Beginning a friendship	13
2	Knowing the promises	24
3	Learning from failure	36
4	Changing our priorities	45
5	Dealing with doubts	55
6	Finding assurance	66
7	Forcing the pace	76
8	Recovering confidence	86
9	Sharing God's heart	98
10	Repeating our mistakes	110
11	Facing sacrifice	119
12	Keeping a perspective	131
	Notes	142

ACKNOWLEDGEMENTS

This book was written in the New England state of Vermont in the autumn of 1984. We want to record our deep gratitude to Harty and Carolyn Gardner, whose generosity in lending us their house led to this opportunity of seeing one of the world's most awesome natural phenomena: autumn leaves in the Green Mountain state. Our warm thanks go also to other friends on both sides of the Atlantic, whose support has made possible a protracted time away from the demands of parish life. I want to say thank you also to Stacy Parrigin, who actually asked to type the manuscript, and made several incisive comments which have been duly incorporated in the text.

Biblical quotations, unless otherwise noted, are from the Revised Standard Version.

INTRODUCTION

My forty-fourth birthday has been very different. First of all, it was also my parents' golden wedding anniversary: a time for grateful celebrations by four sons, other relatives and long-standing family friends; a sense of history, permanence, God's faithfulness and the strength of Christian family life. Yes, forty-four years of security and stability.

On the other hand, it was a very uncertain and insecure occasion. I was without a job – and with nothing settled for the foreseeable future. Our furniture is in a house in Oxford that does not belong to us. Our clothes are in several suitcases awaiting travel to America for a temporary stay in an unknown house in a fairly remote part of the country for an unspecified period of time. Our children have nowhere to call home. I have one address for general correspondence, another address for official correspondence, a third address for personal correspondence.

It is therefore, particularly appropriate that we should be reading *Pilgrim's Progress* by John Bunyan for our family devotions. A birthday card from my younger son depicts a family arriving by car at their destination, where father unpacks an inflatable house and begins to pump it up. My son's written comment reflects both his humour and his insecurity: 'And I hope that we get something better than a ready-to-move inflatable house in the future!!' We have just settled, temporarily, into our eighth house in two months – so his rueful comment is understandable.

If 'mid-life crisis' is more than a catch-phrase pioneered

by psychiatrists, I can begin to understand why I am
feeling rather more vulnerable than usual to all these
uncertainties. I sense more acutely than before the
pilgrim-calling of the Christian. I can identify with
Abraham in his life of pilgrimage once God moved into
his life. I can appreciate a little bit of what those heroes of
Christian biography meant when they talked about living
by faith – people like Francis of Assisi, George Muller,
Hudson Taylor, Mother Teresa.

And then I am reminded of the way some modern
Christians tend to talk and write about 'kingdom faith'
and their own understanding of what it means to live by
faith, to hold on in faith, to ask in faith, to receive by faith.
And I find myself wondering how all these experiences
hold together: Abraham, John Bunyan, St Francis,
Mother Teresa, the missionary heroes of my youth, the
awesome stories of faith and 'success' in much Christian
writing today, and our own experience as a family with a
rich inheritance and an uncertain future. Where is the
common strand? What does it mean to live by faith?

That is the nub of this book. It is, unashamedly, a study
of the life of Abraham. Over the years I have found this Old
Testament character a constant source of encouragement,
sanity and relevance. With so many versions of faith being
marketed, it is particularly important to return to the
person who is called 'the father of all who believe'
(Romans 4:11), so that we form a clearly *biblical* understanding of living by faith. Abraham provides a rounded
portrait of someone manifestly fired by faith in God, but
also riddled with doubt, driven to disobedience and
plagued by fear – like you and me.

Only this week we received a letter from a friend telling
of a Christian couple beginning to cope with the news that
their daughter has developed diabetes: a matter of deep
personal concern – not devastating, but seriously worry-
ing and calling for considerable readjustment, sensitivity
and, yes, faith. But their most stressful problem is more
subtle: how to deal with well-meaning friends who insist

that their daughter's condition has come about through *lack* of faith and will disappear through the exercise of *more* faith.

I have such situations in my mind in this book. I do not think any direct answers to this kind of dilemma will necessarily be forthcoming. But I trust that perspectives will emerge from which we can gain fresh insight from the Scriptures into the life of faith: *Christian* faith in the God and Father of our Lord Jesus Christ.

1 BEGINNING A FRIENDSHIP

There were about sixteen or seventeen people in our sitting room, mostly students. It was the first week of the new academic year; the majority were recent arrivals in Oxford. They had come into touch with Christians and Christianity during their first few days in the city, and here they were in our home, openly sharing what had brought them to that house at that particular stage in their lives. The evening gathering was called a Beginners' Group and, after the initial introduction and inevitable coffee, each one began to explain how they happened to be there.

Each story was different, and I cannot remember them all now, four years on. But I do recall one particular girl. When she was fourteen, her father had walked out of the home (he returned some time later). The shock so shattered his daughter that she took down an old Bible, hitherto unopened, and began to read. She studied the life of Jesus. He became real to her and she began to live out her new and fragile faith at home and at school – but without meeting anyone for four years who seemed remotely on the same wavelength.

Then she came to Oxford. On her first Sunday she was taken to church, where she found seven or eight hundred young people involved in the service and a message proclaimed which gave substance to her own personal faith. You can imagine her joy! During her three years at the university she made great strides in faith, met and recently married a Christian man, and is now witnessing to her faith with steady consistency.

At a more recent gathering of a similar kind, I remember a young garage mechanic in his late twenties, entirely

alien to everything Christian and never even vaguely
linked with a church, speaking out very frankly about 'all
this Christian stuff'. He had been fascinated by the faith of
his girlfriend and simply wanted to know. His inner
struggles as he see-sawed his way to a living faith were
both painful and illuminating. There was clearly no way
in which he could prise himself free from the pursuing
love of God.

There are many such stories – for example, the sixteen-
year-old schoolboy in the same group who, having
recently come to faith in Christ himself, found within
himself a burning concern for his grandfather, a professor
at the university, who was dying of cancer without any
faith; the man was converted virtually on his deathbed.

GOD'S INITIATIVE

One common denominator stands out from every such
biography: God broke into each life in sovereign
initiative. He made himself known to each person in ways
which matched the unique circumstances of every
individual. Their faith was kindled by God's self-
disclosure. True faith is never anything other than the
response of a human being to the initiative of God in
making himself known. Faith never takes the first step: it
responds to God's own grace in revealing himself. This
essential fact about faith is, above every other considera-
tion, the key to living *by* faith. The Christian life begins
with our response to God's initiative, and it continues
with repeated response to God's continued initiatives in
self-disclosure.

I believe there is an *immediacy* about this self-disclosure
by God – an immediacy which alone can and does elicit
true faith. However true it is that God has, once and for all,
revealed himself in history in the life, death and
resurrection of Jesus, it is still necessary for a distinctive
work of God's Spirit to make this mighty 'salvation

history' come alive if any individual is to respond to God's grace with living faith. Moreover, what is true at the beginning of the life of faith remains true throughout the lifelong journey of faith. We move ahead in faith as we sense the Spirit of God making his love, light and truth personally relevant to us now.

So long as this immediacy of both self-disclosure by God and personal faith in the individual is not clearly present, we can beat one another over the head with monotonous urgency as we try to bring about faith for today's discipleship – but we will get nowhere. Why? Because faith can never be manufactured, manipulated or made to order. Faith can only be the willing response of a person who sees God and says 'Here am I'.

Let me stress that this is as true for me today, thirty years on in my Christian discipleship, as it was on that August evening in Somerset in 1955 when I first 'saw' who Jesus is, what he had done for me, what he was expecting of me, and what my response to him both had to be and was now going to be.

This truth shines out brilliantly from God's dealings with Abraham. The Genesis account makes it plain that God came to Abram, as he was then called, out of a clear blue sky. There was no apparent build-up, no shots across the bows, let alone any signs of particular merit in Abraham or significant interest on his part in the Lord. God stepped into the Mesopotamian's life – 'a wandering Aramean was my father' (Deut. 26:5).

It seems likely, as far as we can be precise on the basis of biblical records, that God spoke twice in a sovereignly decisive way: once when Abraham was still in Ur of the Chaldees, and again some years later when he was in Haran – probably after the death of his father, Terah (Gen. 11:31 and Acts 7:2 ff). Terah had decided to emigrate from Ur to the land of Canaan, not on the basis of any divine consciousness or call, but presumably because the Canaanite grass was widely known to be considerably greener than the Chaldean; if you wanted a new life for

your family, then Canaan was reputedly the place to go:
Canaan was the scene of an advanced civilisation, the
theatre of great ethnic movements, a country of walled
cities and numberless unwalled villages, full of the
activities of an extensive international trade. The lure of
Canaan was irresistible.

A HALFWAY HALT

Or almost irresistible. Haran was just over half way
between Ur and Canaan – up and over the top of the Fertile
Crescent, before dropping down southwest towards the
promised land. Terah was happy to settle down in Haran –
and Abraham, with his wife Sarah, was not at that stage
ready to launch out on his own. Neither was Lot, Terah's
grandson and Abraham's nephew.

But when Terah died, God spoke a second time to
Abraham. Originally in Ur God had told him to leave his
land and his kindred for an unknown destination. When
his father had decided to move, Abraham probably
thought it fitted in conveniently with this unprecedented
summons from an unknown God. Perhaps he later
reckoned that Haran was the promised land of destiny,
although the mention of leaving land *and kindred* must
have niggled. This time in Haran the message was unmistakable: 'Go from your country and your kindred and
your father's house to the land that I will show you.'

'So Abram went...' – and the rest of the Genesis
narrative records the ups and downs of the man's life of
faith. We read that 'Lot went with him', thereby setting in
motion not a few difficult and dangerous events. Perhaps
God had intended Lot to be included in his prohibition of
'kindred' as companions on Abraham's pilgrimage of
faith – we do not know for sure.

But the truly remarkable fact is that when the Lord said
'Go', Abraham went. He did not know the Lord. Nobody
in Mesopotamia knew the Lord. God moved into

Abraham's life and challenged him to follow, revealing enough of himself for Abraham to say 'Yes'. The writer to the Hebrews put it with consummate precision: 'By faith Abraham obeyed when he was called to go out to a place which he was to receive as an inheritance; and he went out, not knowing where he was going' (Heb. 11:8).

OBSTACLES TO FAITH

Two specific things strike me about that little cameo of Abraham. He did not know where he was going – a factor which would make most western Christians fidget very uncomfortably, because we invariably want to know both the details and the reasons, as well as the dangers and the advantages, before we will go anywhere. The other factor is easily overlooked in the scant economy of the Genesis account: Abraham was to receive, eventually, a land 'as an inheritance'. But Abraham had no heir to entrust with any inheritance. That was painfully clear: 'The name of Abram's wife was Sarai... Now Sarai was barren; she had no child' (Gen. 11:30).

Abraham and Sarah were not honeymooners. They had wanted and tried to have children for years, but could not: the account records the fact not just once, but – with poignant pointedness – twice in the same sentence. So what was this about an inheritance? A sick joke? 'I will make of you a great nation.... By you shall all the families of the earth be blessed' (Gen. 12:2).

We will come back to the promises of God later. For the moment it is enough to note the ready obedience to which Abraham's new faith in this initiative-seizing God had already moved him – in spite of his ignorance about where he was being taken and in spite of the extraordinarily powerful dissuader presented by his wife's infertility. There were no sophisticated gynaecological resources in Haran in 1984 BC.

We are bound to conclude, therefore, that Abraham's

faith was planted within him by God himself. God had a
unique purpose for his life – which is perhaps the under-
statement to end all understatements! If God chooses to
reveal himself to an individual, he has in that very choice
committed himself to securing effective faith in that
person's discipleship. God's call to Abraham was a call
from nowhere. It was, moreover, a call to go anywhere.

God's call came to Abraham at the precise point of his
own powerlessness, as expressed in Sarah's barrenness.
The call took into realistic account this humanly-
irretrievable situation. God was inviting Abraham to
exercise trust in his ability as God to transcend the
limitations of Abraham's humanness. The call, then, was
based not on Abraham's strengths, but on his known, and
felt, weakness. It was, therefore, a call which emanated
entirely from the grace of God, and was in no sense
dependent on Abraham's abilities. In this crucial sense,
God's call drew forth Abraham's faith in God precisely
because there was no way in which he could have
responded to such a call out of his own resources.

A FAITH FOR EVERYONE

It is possible now – and, I believe, necessary – to see how
God's call to Abraham is a paradigm of his call through
Jesus to any individual. In calling Abraham God
commanded and commissioned him to the obedience of
faith. The call was underscored with specific promises. In
his ready response to God, 'Abraham ... introduces ... a
way of responding to God that is open to all men: that is,
the way of faith.'[1]

We notice also that Abraham was not required to
contribute anything in responding to God's call: 'God
asked him to bring nothing with him but himself; that is,
in one sense, to contribute nothing, and yet, in another
sense, to give everything, and henceforth to be wholly at
God's command.'[2]

In these two basic senses, Abraham is 'the father of all who believe': faith is the way to please God, and there is nothing we can bring to God except our very selves. In Jesus these two fundamentals assume central importance. Later we will pursue how Paul, in particular, expounds this pattern of life in Abraham (especially in Romans 4, Galatians 3 and 4). At this stage we can appreciate with greater understanding the force of a somewhat obscure remark in the epistle to the Hebrews: 'Surely it is not with angels that Jesus is concerned, but with the descendants of Abraham' (Heb. 2:16).

From the outset of his ministry Jesus was conscious of the wrong sense in which many, if not most, of his Jewish contemporaries interpreted the significance of their being descended from Abraham. Indeed, John the Baptist had launched a virulent attack on those Jews who prided themselves on their pure pedigree, when God was requiring each one of them to repent in preparation for the imminent coming of the Messiah: 'You brood of vipers! Who warned you to flee from the wrath to come? Bear fruit that befits repentance, and do not begin to say to yourselves, "We have Abraham as our father"' (Luke 3:7,8).

As the forerunner of Jesus, John was equally concerned with the true descendants of Abraham, a 'family' which had nothing to do with racial purity or religious observance. John articulated the priority of divine initiative in calling men and women to faith: 'I tell you, God is able from these stones to raise up children to Abraham' (Luke 3:8). A person's family background, religious orthodoxy, moral impressiveness or racial origins are quite simply irrelevant to saving faith. Faith is a gift, not a reward or a right.

UNLIKELY PEOPLE

There are two specific incidents in the public ministry of

Jesus which make this point with emphasis. The first describes one of his visits to a local synagogue in Galilee on the sabbath. Seeing a woman who had been bent double for eighteen years, Jesus laid hands on her and healed her – to the angry chagrin of the religious hierarchy, who could not countenance anything unorthodox on the sabbath day, or on any other day, for that matter. Jesus had deliberately stepped into the woman's life with grace and truth, and God was praised as a result. Jesus's own verdict on what had taken place is surely of abiding significance in understanding God's ways with men and women in every generation and culture: 'Ought not this woman, a daughter of Abraham whom Satan bound for eighteen years, be loosed from this bond on the sabbath day?' (Luke 13:10–17).

The initiative of divine grace moving into a situation of human sin and misery is even more apparent in the story of Zacchaeus. The unpopular little tax-collector had heard enough about Jesus to make a considerable effort to see him when he came to Jericho – but I doubt whether he bargained for the grace and truth which Jesus introduced into his life at work and at home on that momentous day. Jesus's own comment on the tax-man's turnaround is fascinating: 'Today salvation has come to this house, since he also is a son of Abraham' (Luke 19:1–10).

In both these cases, whether for reasons of physical infirmity or social ostracism, normal human assessments had written off the two people concerned. Jesus moved into their lives at the point of their greatest and very obvious need – with a glorious demonstration of his gracious power to heal and to deliver, whether from physical infirmity or from moral and spiritual bondage.

We can see, therefore, why the writer of the letter to the Hebrews was so anxious to stress that Jesus was concerned with 'the descendants of Abraham' – not his literal descendants, but those whom God chose to raise up as children to Abraham from the lifeless, stony hardness of physical and moral ugliness. By such acts of grace he drew forth the obedience of faith. To repeat what I wrote earlier, faith can only be the willing response of a person who sees God and says, 'Here am I'.

FAITH AS RESPONSE

It is valuable, at this point, to return directly to Abraham – not to look further at his own response to God, but to discover how God himself, many generations later, described his intervention in the man's life. We find God speaking through Joshua in the twilight of his life to the whole assembled nation of Israel: 'Your fathers lived of old beyond the Euphrates, Terah, the father of Abraham and of Nahor: and they served other gods. Then I took your father Abraham from beyond the River and led him through all the land of Canaan' (Joshua 24:2,3). 'They served other gods.... Then I took Abraham... and led him' – that is divine initiative in all its sovereign grace. Without it there could never be such a thing as faith. Faith is our response to God's self-disclosure as the God of all grace.

There is one obvious and crucial corollary of this truth. We grow in faith, and we help others to grow in faith, not by insisting on the importance of faith, but by dwelling on the grace of God. And if there seems to be a dearth of divine grace in a person's life – our own or anyone else's – our privilege is to pray for the Lord to reveal himself as the God he assuredly is – full of compassion and mercy, who keeps covenant love with his people.

In practical terms this will usually mean withdrawing from people, giving them space to breathe and giving ourselves time to pray for them, and praying appropriately – i.e. that God's grace will be shown to them so that they can embrace it with the faith which God gives whenever he discloses himself to us. It does me personally no good at all to be told that I need more faith. I know I do. I also know that the more I concentrate on the faith I do not have but know I ought to have, the more hopeless and useless I feel. I need to be pointed away from myself to Jesus, who is actually described as 'the author of faith' (Heb. 12:2): faith comes from him as a gift (see Eph. 2:8).

In their extremity, under a deep sense of failure and uselessness, the disciples of Jesus recognised this: 'Lord, increase our faith' (Luke 17:5), they pleaded. In reply he did not talk about any need for vastly increased *amounts* of faith, but about faith of the right kind – faith in God: even faith the size of a grain of mustard seed can move mountains, if it is firmly directed towards God.

FAITH TOWARDS GOD

The need today, as I see it, is to redirect faith back towards God rather than to redouble our efforts to show more faith. 'Abraham believed God, and it was reckoned to him as righteousness' – that is the testimony of Genesis, Romans, Galatians and James (Gen. 15:6; Rom. 4:3; Gal. 3:6; James 2:23). The *amount* of faith is not relevant: it is the *object* of faith that is determinative. What faith may or may not achieve is secondary to the Lord's delight and pleasure in those who exercise it. 'Without faith it is impossible to please him' (Heb. 11:6) and God is looking for righteousness, which begins, continues and is completed with the obedience of faith.

In fact, if we were to look at Abraham's life from the viewpoint of the results which he achieved by his faith, we would be singularly disappointed. God did not seem to be interested in that at all. He was concerned to see a man growing to trust, follow, obey and love him as a friend in all the varied circumstances of his life. The chapters in the book of Genesis that describe the life of Abraham do not list his achievements. If anything, they list his failures. Most importantly, they recount *God's* dealing with Abraham.

We move beyond the proper arena of faith when we

either quantify it or assess its value in utilitarian or pragmatic terms – for example, by counting converts, budgets, worshippers, healings, or even answers to prayer. For Abraham, his faith expressed his friendship with God; for God, Abraham's faith made such friendship possible. Friendship is not measured by what is achieved. Friendship is not measured at all: it is enjoyed, and it is shared, and above everything it deepens and grows. Other people talked about Abraham as God's friend (see 2 Chron. 20:7). What is even more striking is that God describes Abraham as 'My friend' (Is. 41:8).

This magnificent friendship began with God's grace and Abraham's faith – and in the same way it continued to grow. In the following chapters we will trace the ways in which God shared himself with Abraham, and the ways in which Abraham, with a few exceptions, shared himself with God. We will discover that very little in the panorama of human experience remains untouched by this great friendship. Living by faith is not the remote experience of a few high-powered people. Living by faith is friendship with the Lord God Almighty and is the gift of God to all who will receive it.

2 KNOWING THE PROMISES

On 12 October 1968 I made some profound and life-changing promises. Out of all the women throughout the world, one woman heard me vow to take her as my wife, to have and to hold her from that day forward; to love and to cherish her, for better, for worse; for richer, for poorer; in sickness and in health; to do this until death parts us, and to forsake all others. I pledged myself to Rosemary in these uncompromising terms. With these promises I sealed a deep friendship, which continues to grow. Equally, she made the same promises to me, and we each accepted in trust the vows then made for life.

At the time we knew enough about each other to be sure of each other. We trusted each other's promises because we were able to trust each other. Without such mutual trust the promises would have been superficial, if not empty. It is no different in the friendship between God and those whom he calls to be his friends. The firmness of the friendship depends upon the character and the promises of God: both speak of his complete faithfulness. He remains faithful to his word because he cannot deny himself (see 2 Tim. 2:13).

Abraham's friendship with God was securely grounded in God's faithful character and faithful promises. As the one who took the initiative in the friendship, God primed the pump of Abraham's responsive faith. In this chapter we will look more closely at the way God reveals his faithfulness: first, in the names by which he is called and which reveal his character, and second, in the promises which he makes to Abraham, his friend. In conclusion we will note how Abraham disciplined himself to stand

firmly on the unshakable ground of God's faithfulness –
but not without frequent hesitation and the inevitable
schooling of God's persistent checking and correction.

THE CHARACTER OF GOD

There is a gradual unfolding of God's character in the
names by which he is called in the Genesis narrative. On
specific occasions in Abraham's life, as we study them
more closely later, a different aspect of God's character
will come into prominence each time. In essence, the Bible
consistently uses names to denote character. This is as true
of human beings as much as it is of God. As God,
therefore, reveals other aspects of his character, so
Abraham is able to deepen his friendship with God.

The writer of Genesis uses two general titles for God in
his narrative of events. (It is generally considered that these
two names indicate two of the major sources from which
the book of Genesis was composed.) The first is Jahweh, or
Jehovah (normally translated 'the Lord'), and refers to the
personal care of the covenant God. (It is also the name by
which he revealed himself to Moses in the burning bush in
the desert – Ex. 3:1ff.) The other word, Elohim, is a more
general title, referring to the guidance and providence of
the ruler of all nations. We will see later how God's
purposes for Ishmael, as distinct from his purposes for
Isaac, are linked to the name Elohim (Gen. 21:12ff). In
general, God's dealings with Abraham are described both
in terms of personal care from the God of the covenant and
in terms of the purposeful guidance of the God of the
universe. It would be artificial so to stress these two
perspectives that we drive a wedge between them.
Nevertheless, it will become clearer as we proceed that
God's covenant dealings with Abraham and with all his
spiritual descendants are fundamental to steady, growing
faith.

More significant still are the other names by which God

makes himself known in the course of Abraham's life. We can appreciate the accumulated impact of these names in building up a portrait of the Lord simply by listing them: God Most High, maker of heaven and earth (Gen. 14:19); your shield (Gen. 15:1); God Almighty, or the God who suffices (Gen. 17:1); the Judge of all the earth (Gen. 18:25); the Everlasting God (Gen. 21:33); the God of heaven and of the earth (Gen. 24:3). We may legitimately add two further aspects of God's character as revealed to Abraham: he showed himself to be Abraham's personal God – 'I will be God to you and to your descendants after you' (Gen. 17:7). This became so manifestly true that Abraham's servant constantly referred to 'the God of my master Abraham' (Gen. 24:12ff). The other truth about God seared into Abraham's soul was 'The Lord shall provide' – a fact which became enshrined in the name of that cardinal venue on Mount Moriah where Abraham was so radically tested in terms of his faith in God (Gen. 22:14).

GOD'S FRIEND

This God called Abraham his friend. Abraham's faith was founded on the personal love of God in choosing him. The God of Abraham is the God and Father of our Lord Jesus Christ, the only begotten Son of God. The Son of God loved me and gave himself for me. He has chosen me, called me to be his friend, appointed me to go and bear lasting fruit. My faith is founded on the personal love of God for me.

This God made heaven and earth. I look around this part of his world – it is, admittedly, one of the most glorious vistas possible to see the trees in Vermont in New England in the 'fall' – and I tell myself, 'God, who made and preserves all this, is my Friend, and I am his friend!' For some completely inexplicable reason, this God has called and chosen *me*. The only reason he has ever given is that he loves me. When the sheer immensity and raw power of his created universe not only emphasise my tiny insignificance, but tempt me to doubt my personal security, I remind myself that he is God of heaven and of the earth, the Most High God who cannot be taken by surprise or ousted from his throne.

Such a sovereignly powerful God rules with justice as Judge of all the earth. He requires and dispenses justice. He is not baffled by human cruelty and wickedness, either when I am responsible for it myself, or when others threaten me or my family with it. He has undertaken to provide for my needs, and he is enough – the God who is sufficient. He knows and understands my fragility and my vulnerability, and therefore he has promised to be a shield around me. No sudden disaster can obliterate him, or, ultimately, me; no process of history can erode his love and power: he is God from everlasting to everlasting. This God is my God, and, to repeat, he has called me to be his friend because he loves me.

THE LOVE OF GOD

My faith in God grows as I take in more and more this unchanging fact that he loves me, that he has called me to be his friend because he loves me, that he has chosen me because he loves me. He made me because he loves me; he loves me because he made me. There is nothing in me, inherently or potentially, that caused him to love me and to choose me. He loves me because he loves me. He loves me because he has chosen to love me – and he does not change. It is impossible to have anything more certain than this: my friendship with God, his friendship with me, is rooted and grounded in his own eternal character. I am living by faith when I accept this and let it envelop my daily life and pervade my inner being.

It seems crucial to spend time stressing and absorbing this fundamental truth. Time and time again in pastoral ministry it becomes apparent that Christians have not

properly grasped it. I think of many different people who
cannot believe God can love them because of what they
have done – or failed to do. Then there are those who
believe their troubles and ills are a punishment from God
because of their disobedience or lack of faith – and that
God will not love them until they have put things right.
Many others spend their days trying to do the kinds of
things that good Christians ought to do in the hope that
God will love them as a consequence.

For all such people, faith ebbs and flows in proportion
to their own feelings, to their sense of God's presence and
blessing, or to the dictates of conscience. Trusting faith in
the unconditional love of a sovereign God is at a premium
these days.

The best illustration of God's unending and unchanging love remains the love of a father for his children.
No matter what they do or fail to do, I love my four
children. However disobedient, distant or defiant they
may be, I love them. Whatever they may feel or think about
my attitude towards them, I still love them. They may
ignore me, drive me mad, walk out of my life – but I love
them. They do things that make me ashamed and there
have been times when I would gladly – though
momentarily – have disowned them: but I still love them.
There is nothing I can visualise that will make me stop
loving them.

I derive my father's love from the love of my Father God.
All love is from God, and all fatherhood is a reflection,
however pale, of the Father's love in the heart of God. My
love for my children, therefore, helps me to appreciate the
unchanging love of God for me. God wants us to live by
faith in this love he has for us. If we do not *feel* God loves
us – and many Christians do not feel God loves them –
faith will grow as we dwell on the certainty, unchange-
ability and constancy of God's love for us, not as we
examine our own lack of assurance.

I WILL . . . I WILL . . . I WILL

To return to Abraham: God's dealings with him combined a continuing revelation of his nature and character with a steady affirmation of his promises. From the outset, God pledged himself to Abraham in repeated promises. The 'I will's' of the Genesis account stand out with pungency and power: 'I will make of you a great nation, and I will bless you, and I will make your name great... I will bless those who bless you, and him who curses you I will curse' (Gen. 12:2,3).

I find that my children are constantly reminding me of the promises I have made to them: 'Daddy, you promised...' An essential part of my relationship with them revolves around my faithfulness to these promises. If I go back on my word, my friendship with my children is significantly impaired. I suppose that most fathers spend their time wriggling out of rash promises, made perhaps under provocation and not from a willing and generous heart. God's friendship with Abraham was not like that; he freely and joyfully made uncompromising promises to Abraham, which he fully intended to make good. He wanted Abraham to take them with complete seriousness, in the conviction that any promise remaining unfulfilled would certainly reach fulfilment, even if it looked impossible.

And many of God's promises to Abraham looked impossible. In fact, the core promise was humanly impossible because it depended on Abraham having a child, something he and Sarah had signally and sadly failed to do. Faced with such a humanly intractable barrier to the fulfilment of God's promises, Abraham had but two options: either to conclude that God did not keep his word, or that God was able to fulfil his promises, even when humanly speaking it was impossible to do so. The story of Abraham's life is the story of the second option, not so much through Abraham's perseverance in faith as through God's own perseverance in stressing to Abraham his faithfulness.

IN GREATER DETAIL.

God went on repeating his initial promises to Abraham. He provided more details, added further assurance, lent further emphasis – but he never retracted or replaced that initial undertaking. It is worth enumerating the number of times in Genesis God reiterated his original promise: 'To your descendants I will give this land' (12:7); 'all the land which you see I will give to you and to your descendants for ever' (13:15); 'look toward heaven and number the stars if you are able to number them – so shall your descendants be' (15:5); 'your descendants shall be sojourners in a land that is not theirs... and they shall come back here in the fourth generation' (15:13-16); 'to your descendants I give this land' (15:8); 'you shall be the father of a multitude of nations' (17:4); 'Sarah your wife shall bear you a son and you shall call his name Isaac' (17:19); 'I will surely return to you in the spring, and Sarah your wife shall have a son' (18:10); 'through Isaac shall your descendants be named' (21:12); 'because you have not withheld your only son... I will indeed multiply your descendants as the stars of heaven and as the sand which is on the seashore' (22:16,17).

It is not hard to see a progression in the details of God's key promise to Abraham, but in essence he repeated the same promise ten times in the course of Abraham's life as God's friend. He forced Abraham back to that promise time and time again. He insisted that Abraham take his word seriously: if God had said something, then it would happen – it was true. That remains the solid ground for our faith. We live by faith as we lay firm hold on the promises of God. We grow in faith as we patiently hold on to the promises God has made, even though in our path lie long delays, much frustration, many dissuaders and virtual impossiblity.

God's promise to Abraham was actually far more remote and unlikely than any promise he has made to us. Abraham also had far less grounds for faith in God than we do. Perhaps that is why God entered more than once into a solemn covenant with Abraham: to guarantee and endorse the bare promise of his words. For example, we read about the following incident:

> When the sun had gone down and it was dark, behold, a smoking fire pot and a flaming torch passed between the two pieces [i.e. two piles of sacrificed animals]. On that day the Lord made a covenant with Abram, saying, 'To your descendants I give this land, from the river of Egypt to the great river, the river Euphrates.' (Gen. 15:17,18)

Several years later this God-initiated covenant was reaffirmed, this time accompanied by an outward sign on Abraham's body to establish the covenant on his part: the rite of circumcision. This was no new or second covenant: 'It shall be a sign of the covenant between me and you' (Gen. 17:2,7ff). In addition to the physical mark of circumcision, God also changed Abram's name to Abraham to indicate the substantive content of the covenant. Abram means 'exalted father'; Abraham means 'father of a multitude'. The first name need not involve actual fatherhood at all; the second name explicitly looks forward to a vast family (Gen. 17:5).

There was little more that God could do to underscore the total reliability of his promises. He had spoken clearly and specifically to Abraham. He had repeated the promises time and time again. He had initiated a solemn agreement to endorse the promises. He had given Abraham a physical mark to be to him – and indeed literally, *upon* him – an absolute guarantee of his promise. And yet God found one further way of making assurance, not just doubly, but repeatedly, sure. The writer to the Hebrews describes it like this:

I SWEAR BY ALMIGHTY GOD

When God made a promise to Abraham, since he had no one greater by whom to swear, he swore by himself, saying, 'Surely I will bless you and multiply you.' And thus Abraham, having patiently endured, obtained the promise. Men indeed swear by a greater than themselves, and in all their disputes an oath is final for confirmation. So when God desired to show more convincingly to the heirs of the promise the unchangeable character of his purpose, he interposed with an oath, so that through two unchangeable things, in which it is impossible that God should prove false, we might have strong encouragement to seize the hope set before us (Heb. 6:13–18).

God intervened with an oath when Abraham went ahead in faith with his readiness to sacrifice Isaac, the son through whom God's promises were to be fulfilled. The text of the Genesis narrative is explicit: 'By myself I have sworn, says the Lord, because you have not withheld your only son, I will indeed bless you, and I will multiply your descendants' (Gen. 22:16,17).

We have become accustomed to mere men swearing till they are blue in the face that they will do what they have promised – so accustomed that we scarcely take any notice of such oaths. God's oaths are different. He cannot give greater force to his promises by appeal to somebody greater and more trustworthy than himself – and so he does the only thing he can do: he swears by himself. A witness in a court of law takes an oath which begins, 'I swear by Almighty God....' Here we have the unbelievable spectacle of Almighty God swearing by himself, so seriously does he take the need for Abraham to believe and to trust his promises.

TWO UNCHANGEABLE THINGS

Abraham had, then, two unchangeable things on which to base his life of faith: the character of God and the promise of God. The two were of a piece, and one word perfectly describes both: faithfulness. This faithful God established an inviolable covenant with his friend, Abraham. Abraham lived by faith in this God and his word.

We noted earlier that *we* have far more grounds for trusting God than Abraham enjoyed at any stage of his life. And yet, there is an intense longing in God's heart that we, as heirs of the promise he originally made to Abraham, should seize firmly all the good things he has promised to us. He has, therefore, not only made 'precious and very great promises' (2 Peter 1:4) to us, he has also enshrined them in a covenant. The friendship into which God has brought us through Jesus has been sealed with his Son's own blood. The cross of Calvary stands in history as God's pledge of his unquenchable love in the complete forgiveness of our sins, in full adoption into his family as sons and daughters, and in the free gift of his own Spirit to dwell in our hearts. That is the new covenant in Christ's own blood which guarantees – if it was ever needed – the utter reliability of the God who promises: 'I will remember their sins no more... I will be their God and they shall be my people... I will put my law within them and I will write it upon their hearts' (Jer. 31:31ff; cf. Ezek. 36:26ff).

All this undergirds God's promises to us today. Whatever we know from the Scriptures that God has promised, he will assuredly perform. I live by faith in God when I write his promises into the very foundation of my daily life. At the very least this means becoming acquainted with God's promises. I believe it is right and necessary to learn them by heart so that we can rehearse them in time of need. There was a time when it was normal to learn the promises of God. Unfortunately, we now have a generation of Christians, sons and daughters of Abraham, who are often missing out on their privileges through sheer ignorance of the promises of God.

We can gauge how serious this ignorance can become when we read what Peter reckoned to be the value of these promises. He asserts that 'through these you may escape the corruption that is in the world because of passion, and become partakers of the divine nature' (2 Peter 1:4). Not to know and live by faith in the promises of God is to sentence ourselves to all kinds of corruption and to deprive ourselves of what it means to be children of God. We must get back to the promises of God and, through them, to the God of those promises – or perish.

DAILY WORSHIP

How do we live by faith in the promises of a faithful God? What should we do to establish such faith more firmly in our daily lives? Abraham provides the answer. In one sense it is obvious; some might even call it trite or over-pious. But we neglect it at our peril. There is a refrain running through the life of Abraham: 'So he built there an altar to the Lord and called on the name of the Lord' (see Gen. 12:7,8; 13:4,18; 21:33; 22:5).

Abraham formed the discipline of establishing worship at the centre of his life. He made a habit of calling on the name of the Lord. However much he found his friendship with God growing naturally and spontaneously as the years went by, he did not neglect special times set apart for worship – personal and corporate, especially in his family life, wherever home happened to be.

If we allow this disciplined approach to worship to slide, we will very soon find living by faith a matter of nostalgia, not of current experience. Our friendship with God goes stale and, from our side, becomes something of a charade. Perhaps the most important thing we can say about living by faith is that it happens *now*, today. We cannot live by faith in the past or in the future. Living by faith has no past historic tense. Equally, in spite of much modern discussion of the theme, living by faith is not so much anticipation of, as assurance about, the future, practising here and now the presence of the God of time and of eternity. That means *daily* worship: new *every* morning.

Abraham did not find such commitment to God in the present at all easy. As we will see in more detail later, the story of Ishmael is supremely eloquent. Abraham tried to anticipate the future in having a son, Ishmael, by his wife's maid, Hagar. He also tried later to live in the past by pleading with God to regard Ishmael as the promised heir, rather than to accept God's purposes for Isaac through Sarah. The whole Ishmael saga smells of doubt, the flesh, disobedience, and worldly wisdom, with all the inevitable consequences of such behaviour. God wanted Abraham to live by faith in him *now*: the past was the past, and belonged to God; the future was the future, and it equally belonged to God.

Let us, then, focus our attention on the Lord God Almighty, who has revealed his faithfulness to us in the Lord Jesus Christ. Let us receive, imbibe and live out the promises of this faithful God. Let us *today* live by faith in God, calling on his name and claiming his promises.

3 LEARNING FROM FAILURE

He was a young Christian, keen to follow the Lord and determined to marry only another Christian. She was attractive, wiser in the ways of the world and more familiar with the ups and downs of being in love; she too was a committed Christian, facing a difficult struggle to keep the Lord's will uppermost in her heart. The two had found a close friendship. He believed that he was head over heels in love; she was less sure, but did not want to call a premature halt to a promising friendship.

Eventually – and inevitably – he had to face up to the crunch: 'Is this the right one? Should I propose to her? The basic priorities seem to be in place. There is no apparent objection of any fundamental kind. Why not ask her this evening to marry me? I know, there are twelve traffic lights between my home and her home – if they are all green ... I will take that as guidance from God to pop the question (and, of course, she will say Yes!).'

The traffic lights were all green – I am sure some of them were synchronised anyway – and I have no doubt that the driving, subconsciously or deliberately, was paced to catch the lights over that well-worn route. Everything went smoothly and the natural conclusion was: Go ahead. I went ahead (I admit to being the man involved!). I proposed. She accepted. The engagement was announced. Friends and relatives were introduced. The wedding was planned. But then – the friendship began to deteriorate. Eventually, the arrangements were terminated. I had fallen in love with the idea of being in love, and she was the first, painfully but honestly, to admit the non-reality of any basis for marriage.

I tell this story because it seems to encapsulate one of the most common – and most misleading – misunderstandings about the life of faith. In brief, this attitude suggests that when God is in something, everything works out smoothly, without any hitches or complications. All the lights are green. For example, here is a person thinking of some new project, perhaps something comparatively unimportant – like building on an extension at home or buying new clothes: 'If it all works out without any delays or problems, I'll take it that it's the right thing to do.'

IF GOD IS IN IT . . .

Such an attitude becomes more serious when a projected course of action is more significant in terms of the people who will be affected by the decision – for example, a dozen or so Christians thinking of moving away from their local fellowship to establish a new church in the neighbourhood: 'If there are no hitches, we will take it that God wants this to happen.' We have all found ourselves in the situation where we have had to say, 'God clearly wants this to happen because all the hassles have been cleared away, and there have been so many obvious answers to prayer.'

I do not have too many problems with such conclusions, provided that they do not obscure ethical compromise, selfish behaviour and mere wish-fulfilment – i.e. if I want something badly enough, I will, by subtle and not-so-subtle means, make sure that I get it. And in so doing, I can easily fool myself into believing that God wants me to have what I will not countenance being denied.

It is important to nail down any false ideas about the way God acts, because so many Christians seem ready to give their sanction to anything which succeeds. The converse of this is the equally strong tendency to run down or write off anything which presents a problem as being an obvious failure – and therefore, by definition, out of line with God's will. Instead of taking the open-hearted stance of Gamaliel ('If this plan or this undertaking is of men, it will fail; but if it is of God, you will not be able to overthrow them; you might even be found opposing God' (Acts 5:38,39)), we often tend to manipulate people and circumstances to achieve our own wishes.

How can we be sure that God has given us the green light? There is an incident in Abraham's early life as a friend of God that illuminates this thorny problem. We read (Gen. 12:10–20) that 'there was a famine in the land' of the Canaanites, where God had brought him after he had taken his family out of Haran. God had already appeared to him and explicitly stated: 'To your descendants I will give this land' (Gen. 12:7). There is nothing in the text to suggest that, with a severe famine in Canaan, Abraham was wrong to do what he did; he went down to Egypt to sojourn there. He went wrong in what he did when he reached Egypt.

Before we examine his wrongdoing, however, we need to feel the force of the narrative in terms of the assumption that, if things go well, God is automatically in it. So far in the story there has been nothing to suggest that Abraham was particularly wealthy. We read that when he left Haran to move to Canaan, he took with him 'all the possessions which they had gathered' (Gen. 12:5) – but there is no reason to suppose that these were anything more than the average possessions of a nomad.

THE TEST OF ADVERSITY

But when Abraham leaves the severe famine conditions of Canaan, which must have reduced his own supplies considerably, and comes into Egypt, everything begins to go very well for him. 'Pharaoh', we read, 'dealt well with Abram: and he had sheep, oxen, he-asses, menservants, maidservants, she-asses, and camels' (Gen. 12:16) – none of which, apparently, he had known before. By the time Abraham left Egypt, he was 'very rich in cattle, in silver and in gold'. Lot also, his nephew and companion, had 'flocks and herds and tents' (Gen. 13:2,5).

The stay in Egypt was, in other words, extremely successful. Surely God was in it: How could it have been so prosperous otherwise? There had been one or two hiccoughs, but they had been sorted out. The trouble is, of course, that this account of Abraham in Egypt has deliberately excised one or two details. I have omitted one determinative incident which sheds a totally different light on this period of Abraham's life. When we want something badly enough, we exercise the same kind of censorship on the word of God, often without realising it. We blur the edges of moral integrity and compromise our deepest convictions.

Let us return to the Genesis narrative:

When Abram was about to enter Egypt, he said to Sarai his wife, 'I know that you are a woman beautiful to behold; and when the Egyptians see you, they will say, "This is his wife;" then they will kill me, but they will let you live. Say you are my sister, that it may go well with me because of you, and that my life may be spared on your account.' When Abram entered Egypt, the Egyptians saw that the woman was very beautiful. And when the princes of Pharaoh saw her, they praised her to Pharaoh. And the woman was taken into Pharaoh's house. And for her sake he dealt well with Abram; and he had sheep, oxen, he-asses, menservants, maid-servants, she-asses, and camels.

The unexpurgated version is eloquent. We need to consider it in relation to that call from God, accompanied by sure promises, that had become the cornerstone of Abraham's life. God, in calling him, had promised to make of him a great nation, to give him a special land, a great name, and rich blessing. All the families of the earth would be blessed because of him. Was it likely, in the light of such promises, that God would let even a severe famine wipe him out? Once in Egypt, would God allow events and people to bring about his death? Without those promises, both situations were extremely precarious. With them undergirding his whole future life, he had no reason whatever to fear famine or violence.

THE POWER OF FEAR

In other words, Abraham failed to allow the practical significance of God's promises to affect his daily decisions and behaviour. Just before the border-post between Canaan and Egypt, he was faced with a choice: can God be trusted to fulfil his promises in Egypt, or would Abraham need to take precautions to preserve his life? He failed to let the impact of God's word sink into his decision-making. He allowed fear, not faith, to rule.

Fear is always liable to produce attitudes and actions of which we later are deeply ashamed. There is a certain ignominy in Abraham's conversation with his wife; he is not at all concerned for Sarah's integrity or purity or honour. Instead of standing with her as protector and husband, he exposes her to all the indignity of being treated as a non-person, a thing to be exploited for private gratification in a harem. All he is concerned for, in effect, is to save his own skin and to ensure that 'it may go well with me'. So long as he gets what he wants, he does not care if his wife is compromised or demeaned.

In his fear and selfishness, Abraham did not pause long enough to appreciate the family security provided by God's undertaking to make of him a great nation. In the context of his own culture, we are right to stress *this* failure rather than his failure to love Sarah as he ought. Abraham was acting as an archetypal male chauvinist in a culture which was completely chauvinistic; but even that cultural conditioning could have been overcome by faithful obedience to the express word of God. Indeed, if he had operated in Egypt with trusting faith in God, the

Egyptians themselves might well have seen an authentic testimony to the Lord God Almighty. The narrative seems to underline the way Abraham's behaviour endorsed Egyptian attitudes to women as sex-objects – twice, Sarah is referred to simply as 'the woman', not as Sarah (Gen. 12:14,15). When the Lord steps back on to centre-stage, she again becomes Sarah, Abraham's wife (Gen. 23:19).

As it was, Abraham's non-faith led to misery for Pharaoh and his household, followed by a curt dismissal from Egypt of the whole family. As so often happens, the ethical standards of the pagan turn out to be purer than those of the compromising and compromised believer:

> The Lord afflicted Pharaoh and his house with great plagues because of Sarai, Abram's wife. So Pharaoh called Abram and said, 'What is this you have done to me? Why did you not tell me that she was your wife? Why did you say, "She is my sister," so that I took her for my wife? Now then, here is your wife, take her, and be gone.' And Pharaoh gave men orders concerning him; and they set him on the way with his wife and all that he had (Gen. 12:17–20).

Abraham sank to this level because he did not let the promises of a faithful God take possession of his soul at a crucial moment in his life. Yes, he told lies – or at least a half-truth – because Sarah was his step-sister (see Gen. 20:12). He was governed by a very natural fear for his own safety, a fear which led to callous indifference to Sarah's honour and personhood. But, at bottom, he did not trust God in the situation – *this* is what led him into sin. Sin is always an expression of non-faith; it is the inevitable consequence of not trusting God. If Abraham had taken time to stand firm on the promises God had made to him, he would not have sinned against Sarah, Pharaoh, or the Lord. As Paul concisely expressed it in another context: 'Whatever does not proceed from faith is sin' (Rom. 14:23).

TURNING ONE'S BACK ON A FRIEND

It is important to see sin as an expression, a consequence,
of non-faith, because we can then more readily appreciate
sin's primary impact on God. God had called Abraham to
be his friend and had secured this friendship with
unconditional and uninhibited promises. When Abraham
chose to ignore those promises, he was turning his back on
his friend. He was telling God, 'I do not believe you and I
do not trust you.' When we view sin in anything less than
this fully personal way, we are reducing its seriousness
before God. The essential seriousness of sin lies in its
fracturing of the relationship with God into which he has
called us by his grace in Jesus Christ. It is the Father's love
for his children that we trample in the mire.

The inevitable result of behaving like this towards the
Lord is that we affect others with our non-faith. Those
bound closest to us will be the most seriously and
profoundly damaged – as Sarah was by Abraham's
behaviour. But anyone whose lives we touch day by day
will also be adversely affected – as was Pharaoh, together
with any Egyptian involved in Pharaoh's encounter with
Abraham and his relationship with Sarah. The Genesis
narrative may be marked by economy of words, but it
conceals only lightly a rich deposit of truth about God,
about men and women, about the way God wants us to
relate and behave, about the way we end up behaving and
failing to relate if we do not listen to him.

Living by faith, therefore, can never be reduced to the
level of seeing whether everything works out conveniently.
Certain material things may go better with a particular
brand of teeth-rotting cola, but that principle does not
apply to Christian discipleship. At the material level,
things went very well indeed for Abraham in Egypt. At
relational levels – those involving his friendship with
God, his relationship with Sarah, and his testimony before
Pharaoh and the Egyptians – Abraham's time in Egypt
was disastrous. We can enjoy material prosperity and

circumstantial good fortune and remain miles away from God's will for us. The net result of such a combination is personal emptiness and inner frustration.

BACK TO THE BEGINNING

What is the way back? The same route Abraham took: 'He journeyed on from the Negeb as far as Bethel, to the place where his tent had been at the beginning, between Bethel and Ai, to the place where he had made an altar at the first; and there Abram called on the name of the Lord' (Gen. 13:3,4). He retraced his footsteps. He went back to the beginning, back to first principles and right priorities. He re-established worship at the centre of his life, and he began once again to listen to God.

Because this description of worship comes four times in these two chapters, it must be significant that when he is in Egypt, no mention is made of building altars and calling on the name of the Lord. In these early days of his friendship with God, this practice is specifically mentioned – at Shechem, at Bethel and at Hebron; but not in Egypt. Because he let worship slide in Egypt, he let much else slide as well. And so the only way to go was back, back to Bethel where he had made an altar at the first.

It is very hard to re-establish worship, whether on our own or with our marriage partner or with our fellow Christians in the local church, particularly if we have let it go by default over a long period of time. This truth is clear to me as my wife and I attempt to re-establish regular prayer times together. We have not been doing this on any regular basis for a very long time. As I began this very paragraph, the hour arrived when we had previously agreed to stop whatever we were doing and get down to prayer. It was a real struggle for me to put down my pen after the first sentence. I managed it, and the remainder of this paragraph was written half-an-hour later. We trust that this is the beginning of a new phase of praying together as the pivot of our partnership in the Lord.

I am sure that, during my time of worshiplessness in my particular Egypt, I have been guilty of Abraham's wrong attitudes and actions. In less blatant ways than he, I have compromised my wife's integrity with chauvinistic behaviour. I have missed or misused opportunities for bearing clear testimony before unbelievers. I have been very low-key in my friendship with the Lord. I need to go back to my Bethel, to establish a discipline of worship in which I can again call on the Lord, hear his word, appropriate his promises, and do his will. The recent half-hour of prayer with my wife will, I trust, be the beginning of this revived discipline.

4   CHANGING OUR PRIORITIES

If in Egypt Abraham failed radically to live by faith, once he returned to Canaan and had re-established worship of the Lord at the heart of his life, he showed in one particular incident a remarkable degree of faith. It was actually more than a single incident. There was a long build-up over several months, or even years, which led to a crisis decision. This decision was to have far-reaching implications.

The nub of the problem is described in these terms:

> Lot, who went with Abram, also had flocks and herds and tents, so that the land could not support both of them dwelling together: for their possessions were so great that they could not dwell together, and there was strife between the herdsmen of Abram's cattle and the herdsmen of Lot's cattle (Gen. 13:5–7).

Their very wealth brought difficulties which were unknown in more austere days, both in the pilgrim existence from Haran onwards and especially in the famine conditions of earlier years.

This wealth had, of course, begun to accumulate as a result of Abraham's ambivalence in Egypt. It would be a trifle unfair to call them ill-gotten gains, but the taste of dishonesty was difficult to erase. Abraham was faced with a severe test: would he be able to trust God in plenty where he had found it too challenging to trust him in need? Often, of course, the test comes to us in reverse: to preserve the same measure of faith in God when we are well off as when we had relatively little.

Abraham would not countenance a situation of continuing conflict in his family. It was necessary, therefore, for the two men to go their separate ways. We have seen already how self-centred Abraham could be – like most of us – when his future was at stake. Here, however, he seems to have learned from his past failure to be remarkably detached from the call of self-interest. It is worth pausing to consider how he found such detachment in this important situation: on the human level, was it not more than likely that he would lose at least a significant part of the promised land?

LEARNING FROM THE PAST

It is at precisely this point of decision that Abraham appears to have remembered the promise of God that he had chosen to ignore on the threshold of Egypt: God had promised him the land, for his own descendants to possess. Whatever division of the land was decided by the two men, God's promise would be unimpaired. God had promised him not just part of the land, but the whole of it. God's sovereign purposes contained within them the details, and the implications, of the decisions about to be made. Looked at from this perspective, the problem actually presented Abraham with no need either to fret or to manipulate.

Abraham was able, therefore, to show great generosity of spirit in giving his nephew complete freedom to choose any part of the land he wanted. 'Is not the whole land before you? Separate yourself from me. If you take the left hand, I will go to the right; or if you take the right hand, I will go to the left' (Gen. 13:9). Trust in God's faithfulness to his promises gave Abraham space to be a peacemaker, because this trust released him from the need to safeguard his own rights or to secure his own future. He had genuinely learned to live by faith in God over this crucial issue of receiving the promised land.

This magnanimity becomes apparent when we pause to consider what he might have done in this situation. If he had operated in the same fashion as before, Lot would certainly have been sacrificed to Abraham's personal ambitions under the old regime, much as Sarah had been. There are many ways to ensure we get our own way where there is a conflict of interest. Christians are often not much different from anyone else in this regard. Abraham, for example, could have come on strong about his rights as God's chosen instrument as patriarch of the family. He could have been blatantly selfish and said outright: 'I'm taking the best region; you will have to make your way as best you can with the remainder.'

I suppose the way Abraham might have dealt with Lot was with a lot of spiritual gobbledegook along the lines of: 'The Lord has told me that you are to have that and I am to have this' – an approach which effectively stops any sensible discussion, which is usually what is intended.

TRUSTING GOD WITH THE FUTURE

Abraham did none of these things. Because he had apparently learned to trust God with his whole future, he was able to give Lot *carte blanche* to choose whatever he wanted. Abraham must have known from observation, coupled with instinct, that Lot was highly unlikely to consult God about what he should do. Yet, because he had let the significance of God's promise to him sink into his soul, he was able to trust God to guide, or at least to mould, the decisions of someone who, at the time, was probably a stranger to living by faith in God. He resorted to no deception or manipulation (as he had done with Pharaoh in Egypt). He did not pull rank or claim any hotline to God. He trusted the Lord to look after him, his family, and his future.

Abraham's example is extremely important for us today. It is very easy to be less than open with God and

with one another about such decisions. We often decide
something ourselves, then take it to the Lord to get his
imprimatur ('Lord, please bless my decision'). We leave
the prayer room, go to the people affected by our choice,
and affirm: 'The Lord has told me we must do this.' In
reality, we are people who attempt to manipulate God to
accept what we want and have already decided.

We often see this in the life of a local church. I have been
guilty myself of pushing things through the decision-
making processes in order to get my own way. On a very
few occasions I have actually bypassed the proper
channels in order to accelerate a course of action. In each
case I have been able to give convincing reasons for my
personal preferences and for the need for more economical
decision-making – by which I have normally meant
unilaterally by me! It has not been hard, also, to use the
right language to clothe it all in respectable piety.

If I were honest with myself, I would have to admit that
often I pushed things through because I was afraid that my
wishes would be resisted or delayed, if not rejected. I was
less than open with my colleagues and fellows because I
was not properly and quietly confident in God and his
purposes. If we have taken the time to sensitise ourselves to
the mind and heart of God, we do not need to push things
through. In fact, the more I try to discern God's specific
will for my life and the life of the church fellowship to
which I belong, the less confident I am about my own
ability to be sure about what God is saying. On the
contrary, I find myself increasingly wanting to keep open
to all possibilities by being as open as I can be to the
insights, ideas, and convictions of anyone else involved in
the situation.

ADMITTING OUR IGNORANCE

The implications of this openness to God and to one
another for the whole matter of living by faith are fairly

remarkable. Abraham's faith was demonstrated, not by clear certainty about what ought to be done, but by virtual agnosticism and a happy readiness to accept as God's will whatever resulted from Lot's decision. Living by faith is not, therefore, equivalent to unshakable confidence about God's will in each given situation. On the contrary, we are living by faith when we admit our ignorance and our lack of insight into God's will, but trust him to work things through in line with his sovereign purposes and faithful promises.

Abraham had little or no confidence in his own wisdom in such circumstances; that was his salvation, just as Lot's willingness to choose his future by himself proved to be his undoing. The two men had lived long enough in the land of Canaan to know by this stage that the cities of the valley, and Sodom in particular, were attractive commercially but corrupt morally: 'Now the men of Sodom were wicked, great sinners against the Lord' (Gen. 13:13). Lot knew what he was doing when he 'chose for himself all the Jordan valley' – it was fertile but fraught with moral danger for himself and his family. He decided to risk it. Only much later did he come to see what he had brought upon them all by an over-confident exposure of unconsecrated human potential.

I can think of a number of Christian families who, due to unwise parental decisions about moving house, have been similarly exposed to the pressures of paganism without the necessary support of a firmly-based Christian home and of peer group believers (or at least other Christians in a local church). It is a powerful temptation, especially when promotion brings greater affluence, to choose a new home for its prestige or its material comforts without any attention to the proximity and quality of Christian fellowship. To appreciate something of the sadness this can produce, we only have to let the impact of Sodom on Lot's wife and two daughters impinge personally on our own sensitivities. Sodom reached inside their souls so pervasively that, even when they left Sodom,

Sodom did not leave their desires and behaviour. (See chapter 19. The relevant passage in Genesis is 19:24–38.)

Lot wanted the best, but he found the lure of wealth and prosperity too strong for him to be able to live in such an environment with God at the centre of his life. We know that he was greatly distressed by the uninhibited licentiousness which he witnessed day by day in Sodom (see 2 Pet. 2: 7,8). But, even when God made it abundantly plain that Sodom's days – indeed, its very hours – were numbered, we find Lot still ready to play with fire. He eventually escaped the destruction of the city only because the Lord showed him special mercy (Gen. 19:16).

I have been immensely impressed over the years by the uncompromising discipleship of wealthy Christians who have brought great blessing to many people, including my own family. Such friends would be the last to claim immunity from the distinctive force of the temptations awaiting anyone with an abundance of material possessions, but they have shown me that it is more than merely possible to keep God uncompromisingly central in a wealthy milieu.

At the same time I have seen Christians gradually sucked under a morass of ungodly practices, with the inevitable toll on their marriage, their family, their health and their integrity. Lot decided to go it alone in a wealthy but wicked environment. This kind of solitary existence must be avoided at all costs by every Christian, but particularly those involved where there is an abundance of worldly power, prestige, and prosperity.

INCENTIVES TO GO FURTHER

The sequel in Abraham's life is equally instructive. Having based his crucial decision upon the promises of a faithful God, he immediately received from God strong encouragement to press on in the same manner:

The Lord said to Abram, after Lot had separated from him, 'Lift up your eyes, and look from the place where you are, northward and southward and eastward and westward; for all the land which you see I will give to you and to your descendants for ever. I will make your descendants as the dust of the earth; so that if one can count the dust of the earth, your descendants also can be counted. Arise, walk through the length and breadth of the land, for I will give it to you' (Gen. 13:14-17).

His step of faith brought further incentive from God to continue stepping out in faith.

This always seems to be true. If, today, we can take that one action which God is calling us to take, we will find our faith strengthened accordingly. It will not lead to any respite in the life of faith; rather, it will lead to another step . . . and another . . . and another. Living by faith is not essentially taking one vast stride to straddle a huge chasm of impossibilities: it is taking the next step which God calls us to now. The one after that will be plain once this one has been taken.

We have proved this in our own walk with God this year. We had no clue where we should move and minister after five years in Oxford. We did not know even whether we should call a halt to our time in Oxford. Eventually, that terminus became plain, but not our next sphere of ministry. At this particular moment of writing, it is still uncertain. But God has led us clearly into a time of quiet refreshment away from the incessant demands of parish and public ministry. We have taken the considerable (to us) step of thus moving out of explicit pastoral ministry. That has been an act of faith. We believe, sometimes through clenched teeth, that God will make the next arena of ministry plain as we wait patiently for him during this open-ended time of respite.

THE NEXT STEP

Most Christians instinctively want to know more than simply the next step – 'at least, Lord, the one after that,' we plead. Such expectations are actually the opposite of living by faith: we want to know the next-but-one step before we launch out on the next one. Abraham found assurance of God's presence and guidance in faithfully doing the next thing on the agenda. It is no surprise to discover that he immediately 'built an altar to the Lord' in the next place he reached, Hebron (Gen. 13:18).

It was while Abraham was living in Hebron, by the oaks of Mamre, that he heard of an attack on Sodom by an invading army, during which the city was ransacked and Lot captured (Gen. 14:1–13). He could so easily have washed his hands of Lot and done nothing. Instead, he took firm and positive action, rescuing Lot, along with the whole spoils of war intact. Faith, it has been observed, is not quietism – a passive attitude of sitting back on our haunches.

On Abraham's return, the king of Sodom 'went out to meet him at the Valley of Shaveh'. The king's appearance coincided with the arrival of a rather shadowy figure named Melchizedek, who is called 'priest of God Most High'. This double encounter, with the king of a godless city and the priest of God Most High, proved crucial in Abraham's attitude to his possessions, and demonstrated convincingly, if not permanently, that he had learned from the *debacle* in Egypt (Abraham repeated his behaviour in Egypt later on in his life – see Gen. 20:1–18 – discussed in chapter 10.)

When Melchizedek pronounced a special blessing from God on Abraham, Abraham's immediate reaction was to give Melchizedek 'a tenth of everything', i.e. a tenth of all the booty from Sodom which he had re-captured. (Gen. 14:20. For the hidden significance of Melchizedek, see Heb. 7:1ff.) God had abundantly prospered him; he acknowledged the fact by giving away a tenth of what he had gained. Abraham was thus making it plain, especially to the king of Sodom and his retinue, that he owed everything to the Lord.

At the same time Abraham could see which way the wind was blowing. A grateful king was virtually bound to make some generous present to the man who had recovered the booty of Sodom, especially in the first flush of an unexpected retrieval of what he must have reckoned to be gone for ever. But Abraham seems to have recalled how he had allowed himself to become indebted to Pharaoh, king of Egypt, for making him a wealthy man not so long previously. He was on no account going to compromise his commitment to God on this occasion. Pharaoh might have said, and kept on saying, 'I have made Abram rich.' To have given a pagan king such leverage rankled with the newly-determined man of faith. And so he uncompromisingly rejected any course of action which could conceivably have brought him under the influence of the king of Sodom: 'I will take nothing . . . I have sworn to the Lord God Most High, maker of heaven and earth, that I would not take a thread or a sandal-thong or anything that is yours, lest you should say, "I have made Abram rich"' (Gen. 14:22,23).

INDEPENDENCE CELEBRATIONS

By these two acts of self-denial, which were actually joyful celebrations of independence from the grip of material possessions, Abraham once again embedded faith in the faithful God into his inner being and daily lifestyle. He gave away a tenth of what he had received through the blessing of God, and the remainder he returned to the king of Sodom. So Abraham gained nothing from the whole enterprise except the joy of seeing Lot rescued, the joy of seeing God at work, and the joy of knowing he was free from the grip of covetousness. When we choose, in reliance on God and his promises, to have these surpassing joys rather than all the assumed happiness of worldly prosperity, we are living by faith.

There will be similar times for all God's friends, when it will require faith to refuse the generous offers which grateful unbelievers may press upon us. The temptation is to see such gifts as the legitimate reward for living by faith. When we begin to think like that, we can easily slip into an attitude that virtually sponges off those whose guilty conscience it is simple to exploit for our own personal gain. To soak the rich in this pseudo-spiritual way is not living by faith. To claim that God meets our needs, as we pray and pressurise the wealthy, is a parody of the trust at the heart of Abraham's life. He trusted God, not for a prosperous lifestyle, but for a promised heir. Abraham's lifestyle was a vivid pointer to his true heart's desire – as the writer to the Hebrews expressed it: 'By faith he sojourned in the land of promise, as in a foreign land, living in tents ... for he looked forward to the city which has foundations, whose builder and maker is God' (Heb. 11:9,10).

In brief summary of Abraham's changed attitude to earthly possessions, we can simply say this: when he could have taken, he chose to give. Such a giver reflects the heart of God himself, who so loved the world that he gave his only Son. Abraham, in this new-found generosity, revealed more directly than at any stage so far that he was close to the heart of God – his friendship with God was rubbing off on his attitudes, motives and priorities. Such a friendship always will make itself known in these life-changing ways.

5   DEALING WITH DOUBTS

The poet Tennyson paints an eloquent picture of the way
faith and doubt are so closely intertwined:

> He fought his doubts and gathered strength,
>   He would not make his judgement blind.
>   He faced the spectres of the mind
> And laid them; thus he came at length
> To find a stronger faith his own.
>
> *(In Memoriam*, XCVI)

The unclouded skies where no darkening storm
threatens and the sun always shines may be the
questionable privilege of a few rare believers. Normally,
however, our faith is hewn out from the rocky ground of
gnawing doubts and fears. Just as the bravest heroes are
those who have fought the fiercest battle against raw
cowardice, so the mightiest acts of faith have been
demonstrated in the furnace of doubt.

Time and again this is proved triumphantly true in the
lives of ordinary men and women. I recall several families
in South Africa who put all their possessions at God's
disposal in response to his call to train for the ordained
ministry of the church. They went through agonies of
doubt, but kept on trusting in the Lord's faithfulness. In
almost every such case, the provision the families needed
was forthcoming only at the eleventh hour, thus keeping
them on tenterhooks.

Then I think of a businesswoman, faced with the
eroding demands of a completely unreasonable, if not
obsessive, senior partner whose only aim in life was

greater profits and their consequent implications in terms of working hours, unquestioning loyalty, and un-complaining sacrifice of effort and health. Should she stand up to him in the name of God, risking the inevitable icy atmosphere and even dismissal? Was she being unreasonable and over-sensitive? Any outsider could see the damaging toll being taken on her health and on the rest of her life. But outsiders often can see these things, without being able to affect the agony of the inner conflict in a conscientious Christian. In the midst of her doubts, she took the step of faith, and a different atmosphere and attitude began to be established in the office – not without much more difficulty and the need for continual reminders.

Another situation comes to mind. This couple had long hoped for a child, but without success. Unable medically to have children, they had become involved in the lengthy, searching and often frustrating process of applying for adoption. At last they received a very beautiful baby girl, amidst particularly unusual circumstances which indi-cated in a very personal way how clearly this was God's special gift to them. Not long after, the little girl became extremely ill. The prognosis was not good. Much prayer was made – by parents, friends, fellow Christians in their local church, and in their home group. The parents became increasingly convinced that they should bring her for special prayer at one of the main Sunday services. It seemed right to choose one of the bi-monthly family services, where the children of the church family would all be present and involved.

That was when doubts and fears began to take over. What if she were not healed? Was it right to involve the whole church in their personal need? Were they not in danger of causing the faith of other children to falter? Anyone who has been in a similar situation will know the way these thoughts, not merely flash into our minds, but can become all-absorbing. Doubt seems to squeeze out any residual faith. But this couple fought through those 'spectres of the mind', brought their daughter to the front of the church for prayer, saw other children riveted by the need and totally convinced that God would heal her – with the result that she was fully healed, the whole church greatly strengthened in faith, and the Lord's name glorified.

DOUBTS AND UNBELIEF

Living by faith involves living with doubt and fear. Abraham discovered this in his own situation. We need to make a careful distinction at this stage: doubt and fear are inevitable and necessary for the nurture of faith, but there is no virtue in them. God had to confront Abraham with his doubts and to command him not to be afraid. However much it is true that our doubts and our fears provide the springboard for positive faith, we must not gloss over their essential origin in unbelief.

We do not, therefore, pretend that the doubts and the fears are not there, lurking around beneath the surface. Equally, we do not play around with them or pander to them. We look them straight in the eye, call them by their proper names, acknowledge their strength, take the Lord's authority over them – and step out in faith. This faith is not positive thinking against the negative feelings of doubt and fear: it is personal trust in the Lord God Almighty, drawing on his resources and banking on his promises. Doubt and fear are enemies of faith – its opposites, not its raw material; obstacles to, not ingredients of, truth. Agnosticism is proper where God has given no clear revelation of the truth: where he has made himself known, agnosticism is unbelief – no more, no less.

Abraham found out that God wanted him to face up honestly to the fears in his own heart and to deal with them. We are given a very succinct example in the wake of his extremely strong witness to faith in God with

Melchizedek and the king of Sodom. 'After these things the word of the Lord came to Abram in a vision, "Fear not, Abram, I am your shield; your reward shall be very great"' (Gen. 15:1).

'Who said I was afraid?' There has been no mention of any fear in Abraham in the narrative. Is this 'Fear not' simply God's way of catching his attention – rather like 'I say, Abram...'? The terse command is so common throughout the Bible that it is easy to miss its force. Fear was unknown before the Fall. Once Adam and Eve had disobeyed God, fear became common and inevitable: 'I was afraid... and I hid myself' (Gen. 3:10). Now, with his friend Abraham, God wants to eliminate fear – this is the first time 'Fear not' appears in the Bible. It is extremely important, especially as it follows – apparently haphazardly – from Abraham's example of faith at the end of the previous chapter.

REACTION AFTER BLESSING

I think it is reasonable to assume that Abraham had just begun to register the significance of what he had done in turning down the offer of great wealth from the king of Sodom. 'What have I just missed? Security for life? Am I mad? Perhaps God wanted me to take it after all?' Abraham had gone out on a limb because he acted in faith, faith in a God whose heart he was beginning to understand by virtue of their growing friendship. There usually seems to be some such reaction after an important step of faith: doubt and fear press in again.

The Lord knew that. And so he forces Abraham to face up to these emerging fears – not solely by a word of command which calls them by their proper name, but with a new revelation of his personal care and protection – 'I am your shield.' This is followed by another specific promise, manifestly linked to Abraham's rejection of any reward for his services from the king of Sodom – 'Your reward shall be very great.'

This three-part statement contains the kernel of what it means to live by faith – a command from God, a declaration by God about himself, and a promise: 'Fear not, I am your shield; your reward shall be very great.' God has his own wise ways of communicating what he wants personally to each of his friends. He knew where and how to touch Abraham. In that sense this statement in Gen. 15:1 is highly personalised and localised in the life of one particular person at one particular time in history.

The principles, however, hold good for every Christian. Discipleship is a matter of 'the obedience of faith' (see Rom. 1:5; 16:26), as both Jesus and Paul constantly make plain. Living by faith is a matter of obeying God, knowing God and trusting God. Different traditions in Christianity tend to stress a different aspect of these three elements, often with the effect of downplaying, if not denying, the importance of the other two. Holding all three in balance keeps us walking ahead in faith.

God's declaration to Abraham, 'I am your shield,' was a fresh revelation of his faithfulness. It is possible that this metaphor from the battlefield is directly linked with Abraham's recent exploits with the raiders of Sodom and Gomorrah, perhaps even a veiled prohibition against any need for a friend of God to take up weapons or use violence either in pursuit of justice or in self-defence: 'I am your shield.' We do not hereafter read of Abraham – or Isaac or Jacob or Joseph – acting in such a manner. Part of what it meant for Abraham to live by faith was to trust the Lord alone for protection from harm and danger – to fight his battles for him, rather according to the pattern spelt out later by Moses at the crossing of the Red Sea: 'Fear not, stand firm, and see the salvation of the Lord, which he will work for you today.... The Lord will fight for you, and you have only to be still' (Ex. 14:13,14).

The Exodus narrative is adamant that such an attitude of trust does not mean passivity, because we immediately read, 'The Lord said to Moses, "Why do you cry to me? Tell the people of Israel to go forward. Lift up your rod, and stretch out your hand over the sea and divide it."'

Hardly passivity! Rather, we see a firm trust in God, coupled with specific steps of faith.

DESCENDING INTO DISILLUSIONMENT

When we return to the account of Abraham, in his response to God's fresh revelation of his protection and his explicit expansion of his promise, we discover a crisis of doubt beginning to seize his soul. The yo-yo experience of faith/doubt is nowhere more plain: 'But Abram said, "O Lord God, what wilt thou give me, for I continue childless and the heir of my house is Eliezer of Damascus? Behold, thou hast given me no offspring; and a slave born in my house will be my heir"' (Gen. 15:2,3).

In other words, Abraham is telling God, 'Look Lord, you say you are going to give me the world; you say you are going to give me this land to possess; you say you are going to give this land to my descendants for ever and ever. And yet nothing is happening. In fact, in terms of anything that really matters, you have given me precisely nothing: you are not a giving God at all.' Abraham reckoned that God had stopped giving. Instead, he reckoned that God did not want to give. He had reached the stage where he believed that God had given him nothing at all.

When doubt and fear take possession of our hearts, we can easily reach the same place as Abraham. We become so disillusioned that we no longer believe that God is a giving God. On the contrary, we conclude that he is a withholding God, a restricting God, a prohibiting God, a condemning God. We suspect that he wants to strip us of everything we enjoy and really want. We cannot bring ourselves any more to believe that God, in his very heart and eternal nature, gives and gives and gives.

Abraham at this point had taken on board the original lie about God. In the story of the serpent deceiving Adam and Eve in the Garden of Eden, the first words spoken through the serpent called into question the generosity and the giving heart of God. The Lord had told them: 'You may freely eat of every tree of the garden, but of the tree of the knowledge of good and evil you shall not eat.' The serpent comes to Eve and says, 'Did God say, "You shall not eat of any tree of the garden"?' No, he certainly did not say that; but by merely suggesting that he had, the character of God had already been misrepresented as niggardly and negative. Indeed, Eve at once revealed that she had lost a clear vision of God in simply paying attention to the serpent's insinuations: she contradicts his suggestions but, in quoting what God had actually said, she omits a vital word: 'We may eat of the fruit of the trees of the garden.' The word left out is 'freely', a key word to describe the lavish generosity of a loving Father God.

THE SOURCE OF LIES

If we find ourselves at the point where, like Abraham, we no longer can believe in God's desire to give and to bless us with his grace, it is important to recognise the nature and the source of this lie. Jesus was uncompromising in his exposure of such lies about God and the way he loves to give himself to men and women. Intriguingly, this exposure comes in the middle of a confrontation with some smug Jews who reckoned they were God's exclusive favourites because 'Abraham is our father'. In their pride and prejudice, they were misrepresenting the character of God and rejecting the gift of God in himself as Messiah. So Jesus bluntly asserts: 'You are of your father, the devil, and your will is to do your father's desires. He was a murderer from the beginning, and has nothing to do with the truth, because there is no truth in him. When he lies, he speaks according to his own nature, for he is a liar and the father of lies' (John 8:31ff).

God has revealed the truth about himself in Jesus. Any description of God's nature which is not in line with the revelation brought by Jesus is a lie. Wrong, false ideas about the nature of God are not simply the coinage and trademark of certain theologians and teachers; they insinuate themselves into the fabric of our relationship with God if we allow them any leeway. Abraham had done so and, for a short time, doubt ejected faith. His friendship with God was temporarily clouded with mistrust and recrimination.

How does God respond? Anyone who knows the pit of doubt and despair will testify to the impossibility of dragging ourselves out by a song and a prayer. *God* has to do something, or we sink even lower. God acted with precision in Abraham's case: 'And, behold, the word of the Lord came to him, "This man shall not be your heir; your own son shall be your heir"' (Gen. 15:4). God nailed the lie with words of one syllable (I don't know Hebrew!). He took Abraham back to his original promise. But he did not simply repeat the same old words. He spelt it out that much more clearly. This was the same promise, but a new, and crucial, detail was added: 'Your own son shall be your heir.'

Now the details of the original promise, with its subsequent riders and repetitions, had always assumed the gift of a son to Abraham – but had never actually said so in as many words. The language used had spoken of descendants, a great nation, all the families of the earth. But this was the first time God had expressly mentioned a son. Theoretically, there were other ways in which the promise might conceivably be fulfilled; but they were very remote, and Abraham at any rate assumed a son was intended. Later we discover that he had the bright idea, or so he thought on Sarah's instigation, that perhaps the son might come through another woman and not through Sarah (Gen. 16:2).

A CLEAR WORD FROM GOD

So Abraham received a clear and fresh word from the Lord,

a word which was completely consistent with all that he had come to know of God's will and ways, a word which, without any padding, addressed his spiritual condition; a word which, in a no-nonsense directness, confronted his self-pity and loss of touch with reality. If we share Abraham's experience of doubting the love of God for us, let us pray, and ask others to pray, for an equally effective word from God. It will not be any startlingly new revelation; it will be a fresh, personal word which makes what God has already revealed – in Jesus the living Word through the written word of the Scriptures – come home with new impact.

God also gave Abraham a visual aid. 'He brought him outside' – had he been locked away in his tent for too long, introspective and wrapped up in himself? – 'and said, "Look toward heaven, and number the stars, if you are able to number them"' (Gen. 15:5). Abraham needed to look away from himself. In the apparently paradoxical way in which God's truth often seems to impinge itself upon our lives, he needed to feel again the vastness of the created universe and his own midget vulnerability – to be reminded that the Lord God Most High is 'the maker of heaven and earth' (Gen. 14:22), as he had only recently declared to the king of Sodom. In that experience of personal smallness, Abraham was assured of his significance and his destiny: 'So shall your descendants be' – as numerous as the stars of heaven, all descended from your own son.

A specific word, a sense of his smallness, an assurance of his significance before God: these were the three ways in which the Lord responded to Abraham's doubts and fears. There was still one important step for him to take to make these things his own, and Abraham took it: 'And he believed the Lord, and he reckoned it to him as righteousness' (Gen. 15:6).

This act of faith is taken, in several seminal passages of the New Testament, as the essence of our response to the Christian gospel. To those in Galatia who had slipped back into seeing their good deeds as the way to win God's approval and become righteous, Paul passionately presents the example of Abraham (Gal. 3 and 4): 'an act of faith accepting God's favour is a very different thing from a work done for the sake of winning God's favour'.[1] Abraham was responding in sheer gratitude to God's initiative in calling him, leading him, forgiving him, protecting him, enabling him, and now lifting him out of the miry clay and putting a new song in his mouth (see Ps. 40:1–3).

His friendship with God was thus restored to its openness and trust. There would be many more doubts, more fear, more failure, more disobedience. But an important, if not determinative, watershed had been passed. He had been on the brink of a lethal marshland, where he would have endlessly struggled to please a God who seemed out to reduce him to a cipher. This bog is one into which many Christians fall directly or gradually, often imperceptibly. It is also one from which the Lord has rescued countless Christians – and wants to rescue everyone.

The nub of Abraham's life hereafter is magnificently expressed by Paul in a passage in his letter to the Romans. It is worth our while allowing the full force of the apostle's words to sink into our hearts, to become engraved in our memories:

> The promise was based on faith, in order that the promise should be guaranteed as God's free gift to all of Abraham's descendants... to those who believe as Abraham did. For Abraham is the spiritual father of us all. So the promise is good in the sight of God, in whom Abraham believed – the God who brings the dead to life and whose command brings into being what did not exist. Abraham believed and hoped, even when there was no reason for hoping, and so became 'the father of many nations....' His faith did not leave him, and he did not doubt God's promise: his faith filled him with

power, and he gave praise to God. He was absolutely sure that God would be able to do what he had promised. That is why Abraham, through faith, 'was accepted as righteous before God' (Rom. 4:16–22).

6 FINDING ASSURANCE

'How can I know that God wants me to go overseas?' She was an attractive girl in her late twenties, unmarried and unattached, a very capable and respected midwife, with considerable experience in Christian ministry. For some time she had felt a pull to serve God in Africa, not least because she had been drawn by the example of a lifetime spent there by an aunt in charge of a hospital. But how was she to know that it was right to go?

Here is another Christian, a businessman with a lovely wife and three young children. His career is well-established with a bank; he is fully involved in active ministry in his local church. His wife too takes a full part in Christian service. The doors are opening for them in all kinds of directions if they stay where they are. But out of the blue comes an offer to move to another part of the country, with uncertain prospects, separation from relatives, uprooting of children, and no apparent church fellowship of equivalent vitality. Every obvious argument tells them to say No, but that persistent niggle will not go away. How can they know what decision is right?

Or take the case of a middle-aged man, made redundant after several years in an executive position and now beginning to taste the emptiness of unemployment and the dehumanisation of being persistently turned down – and often finding his letters completely ignored and unanswered. On top of all this, his marriage has foundered and his health is uncertain. After months of useless job-hunting, somebody suggests he turn his hand to teaching, which he has never done before and never even considered. It means further training, and no guarantee of eventual employment in a career already heavily over-populated. How is he to know that this is right?

Any minister of a church could give endless such stories. I suppose the theme of guidance – knowing what God wants for us – is the most common problem brought to us. I have chosen the above examples because each one involved a radical change of direction, the issues of which affected the whole way of life to be followed by the individuals concerned and by several people linked with them.

NO INFALLIBLE FORMULA

There is certainly no fail-safe method of ensuring that we travel God's route for us, no formula for guaranteeing infallibility. In fact, the more I live as a Christian, the more uncertain I seem to become about my decision-making. The issues seem more, rather than less, complicated. The possibilities seem to increase to present a multiplicity of options – and that makes decisions more difficult.

At the same time, I am beginning to see that it may not be as crucial as I have hitherto believed to reach 100 per cent assurance about God's detailed will for my life; perhaps I am not meant to be absolutely sure. Yes, I would like to be sure about all kinds of things. But maybe the fact that I remain strangely in the dark, even after long waiting and much prayer, shows that God might even intend me to be uncertain. I can see now that there are many things it is better that I do not know.

In that connection, I can think in retrospect of several details concerning our ministry in Oxford, Cape Town and Reigate which were withheld from us when we were pondering the possibility of going to each one of the three churches. If I had known beforehand about those things, I am fairly sure I would not have gone. In each case there remained a substantial element of uncertainty before our moving into the situation.

On reflection, I must stress also that amidst the uncertainty, we did receive as much certainty as we needed to make us decide to go. It is clear, however, that the uncertainty was as important as the certainty: the imponderables emphasised the need to trust in the Lord and not to be self-reliant.

More than that can be said. The times, often protracted, when I have been kept in uncertainty about the future, have been full of instruction from the Lord. In this sense, the times of uncertainty have been as significant as the moment of clarity and decision-making. During these times, I have come to know the Lord better; I have come to know myself better; I have come to know my family better because I have had to spend more effort sharing their uncertainties and sensing their feelings; and I have come to know my fellow Christians better because we have been thrown together more as we have shared our uncertainties.

For all these reasons I find myself completely at one with Abraham when he turns to the Lord and says, 'O Lord God, how am I to know that I shall possess the land?' (Gen. 15:8). The timing of this heartfelt expostulation is highly significant. As we saw in the last chapter, he has just negotiated a crisis of doubt and faith; he has come out of a deep pit of negativity and virtual unbelief. God has both reiterated his original promise and spelt it out unambiguously: 'And he believed the Lord.'

As always, God responded to Abraham's new step of faith with another declaration of his intent: 'I am the Lord who brought you from Ur of the Chaldeans, to give you this land to possess' (Gen. 15:7). This emphasis on God's original call way back in Mesopotamia was probably intended to make Abraham pause to think: 'God has been with me from the outset, a thousand miles away and thirty years ago; he is not going to leave me in the lurch now.'

THE DOUBTS WHICH NIGGLE

But Abraham wanted to know. The promise of God, the nature of God, and the track record of God's dealings with him over the years – none of these could totally remove the man's niggling doubts. He wanted further assurance. Rather like Gideon with his fleece (see Judges 6:36–40), Abraham 'asked for some confirmatory pledge to be added to the bare word of God'.[1]

I am extremely relieved that, in his patience and understanding, the Lord is prepared to indulge such personal foibles in his people. In essence they are nothing but doubt dressed up as humble requests – 'so that I don't make a mistake, Lord, and let you down.' But all the way through the Bible the Lord can be seen meeting this kind of ambivalence with further indications of his blessing and guidance: Moses with his shopping list of excuses (Ex. 3:11–4:7); Elijah wallowing in self-pity in the total exhaustion which followed his Carmel confrontation with the prophets of Baal (1 Kings 19:1–18); Isaiah and Jeremiah properly overawed by the scope of their commission (Is. 6:1–13; Jer. 1:1–12); Amos explaining that farmers might not make the best prophets (Amos 7:14); Jonah using every trick in the book to evade God's commands (Jonah 1:1–3; 4:1–11); and Peter advocating to the Lord much better ways of going about his mission (Mt. 16:21–3; John 18:10,11; Acts 10:9–16).

The Lord was patient with each one – give or take the odd touch of exasperation and the occasional straight rebuke. I must admit that I think I would have blown my top with Moses: he really scraped the barrel in his attempts to stave off God's call. And yet I am just like Moses in the excuses I come up with to avoid the next step of faith. I also like to have the future mapped out, to hedge my bets, to make assurance *doubly* sure, and would prefer that the Lord send someone else. And I am both amazed and grateful that the Lord is so patient with us: he clearly means business. He has called me; he is faithful; he *will* do it (1 Thess. 5:24).

PERSONAL FOIBLES

What I have discovered is that the Lord knows the way I
need to receive his assurance. He knows the factors which
weigh uppermost in my mind in making important
decisions. He knows how to get through to me in the midst
of my doubts and fears so that I am sufficiently clear to
move forward in faith. He knows the best methods of
communicating his will to me. Although over the years I
may have grown more rather than less tentative about
laying claim to total conviction about God's will, I have
nevertheless grown in my friendship with him, because
the Guide is more important to me than the guidance. As
this friendship has grown I have become better able to
discern his voice amidst the cacophony of human voices
around me: I can recognise the voice of the good Shepherd
(John 10:4,5,15,16,27).

I discover from other parts of the Scriptures that the
bottom line of guidance is this friendship with the Lord,
not dreams or visions or words of prophecy or specific
verses from the Bible. All or any of these may be used as
instruments, but we dare not let them take the place of a
growing friendship with God. David discovered this, and
he takes great care to share his discovery in Psalm 25:

Good and upright is the Lord; therefore he instructs
sinners in the way. He leads the humble in what is right,
and teaches the humble his way. All the paths of the
Lord are steadfast love and faithfulness, for those who
keep his covenant and his testimonies.... Who is the
man that fears the Lord? Him will he instruct in the way
that he should choose.... The friendship of the Lord is
for those who fear him, and he makes known to them his
covenant.

Each person is unique and distinctive, intrinsically
special in the eyes of God. He alone knows how we tick.
Each Christian's friendship with the Lord is, therefore,

unique. He communicates his will to each person in line with his or her idiosyncrasies. He created us, and thus he alone can, in friendship, respect our individuality and release our potential. The way he communicates to you will be different from the way he communicates to me. Nobody should feel cheated if others seem to get more transparent and striking guidance; they need it in order to be up and doing. Because I am slow to respond to the Lord's promptings and because he knows that I need unmistakable directions, the Lord has graciously given me over the years some very clear guidance. Others do not need the writing in the sky.

I offer a personal example here. As the final year of my training for ordination began, I was anxious about two intertwined matters: where I should serve my first curacy, and how I was going to cope as a clergyman with a pronounced stammer. Others close to me were very worried about the stammer; they seriously questioned whether I should be ordained. My college principal suggested some fairly radical psychotherapy in an attempt to improve the situation. After much prayer, I decided not to have it because I felt that the Lord intended to look after the stammer without, in this case, human resources. I think at that stage I had also reached the point of recognising the stammer as a valuable weakness, if it ingrained in me my dependence on the grace of God. I would now add my growing conviction that effective ministry is, in any case, not a question of the absence of personal weakness.

I still had to decide where to go for my curacy. There were several possibilities. I explored two, and they proved unsuitable. I then went to spend the weekend at Reigate Parish Church just before Christmas 1966 – just after making my decision not to have treatment for the stammer – but still feeling vulnerable and uncertain. Imagine my surprise and delight when the appointed Old Testament reading began: 'Behold, a king shall reign in righteous-ness.... And the tongue of the stammerers will speak readily and distinctly' (Is. 32:1-4). I went to Reigate.

The Lord knows how to build up our faith, especially when it is riddled with doubt. But to return to Abraham at this stage of fresh uncertainty in his life: the Lord dealt with him precisely as Abraham needed. The details are extremely instructive, not so much in their specifics as in the principles underlying them (Gen. 15:9-21).

STRANGE INSTRUCTIONS

First, we again notice that God does not rebuke Abraham for his request. He gives him instructions – strange instructions, as they seem to us: 'Bring me a heifer three years old, a she-goat three years old, a ram three years old, a turtledove, and a pigeon.' Abraham seemed to know what to do: 'He brought him all these, cut them in two, and laid each half over against the other; but he did not cut the birds in two. And when birds of prey came down upon the carcasses, Abram drove them away.'

I don't know about you, but such instructions would have been entirely wasted on me. I'm still not sure what a heifer is, I can't tell the difference between a turtledove and a pigeon, you wouldn't catch me cutting any animal in two, and I'm scared stiff of birds of prey. The Lord knew how to communicate with Abraham and the Lord knows how to communicate with you and with me. We are all different. When Abraham received these instructions, so suitable for him, he obeyed. Do we?

These very specific instructions to Abraham were the prelude to a remarkable demonstration by God of his irreversible commitment to give the land of Canaan to Abraham's descendants for ever: 'On that day the Lord made a covenant with Abram' (Gen. 15:18). The business with the animals was linked with this covenant: 'When the sun had gone down and it was dark, behold, a smoking firepot and a flaming torch passed between these pieces' (i.e. of the animals Abraham had slaughtered and cut in two). Apparently, light passing between the divided pieces of slain animals was integral to 'the customary ritual for sealing a covenant'.[2] In his own culture and generation, Abraham knew exactly what God was doing and what God meant.

THE PROMISE SEALED

So the Lord's oft-repeated promise to Abraham was sealed in dramatic fashion with this covenant: 'To your descendants I give this land' – the actual tense of the verb seems to underline the new dimension in God's sovereign purposes. Hitherto, the promise has consistently been articulated in the future tense. Now the Lord moves into the present tense, or even, as some translations and commentators stress, into the perfect tense: 'I have given you this land.' 'On God's side ... the "giving" was already done; and God thereby pledged himself to bring about possession, and to cause Abraham's descendants to inherit the land.'[3]

In case Abraham had any further doubts – perhaps even to anticipate them – the Lord even drew a map for him, a map with physical geography ('from the river of Egypt to the great river, the river Euphrates' – Gen. 15:18) and with political geography ('the land of the Kenites, the Kenizzites, the Kadmonites, the Hittites, the Perizzites, the Rephaim, the Amorites, the Canaanites, the Girgashites and the Jebusites' – Gen. 15:19-21). All the time the Lord stretched Abraham's faith, not by criticising him for his doubts, but by expanding his appreciation of his own promises and attention to detail. God directed Abraham away from his doubts to God's purposes and promises.

There is, however, in this drama a very important further incident. It took place after Abraham had killed the animals and before the Lord made the covenant with him. 'As the sun was going down, a deep sleep fell on Abram; and lo, a dread and great darkness fell upon him'

(Gen. 15:12). Abraham had asked God to give him
assurance about the future. But the future was not all
sweetness and light. It included periods of deep darkness.
In his sleep Abraham was shown something of this
darkness in a very painful way. His descendants would
have to endure miserable slavery in a foreign land for over
400 years before returning 'with great possessions' to
Canaan. He himself would be spared that suffering: 'You
shall go to your fathers in peace; you shall be buried in a
good old age.'

SHARING GOD'S SUFFERING

I see here a most important principle in God's ways with
his friends: to be assured of God's will for us involves
entering into the suffering of his people and, indeed, into
God's own sufferings in his identification with his people.
This involvement in suffering sometimes comes in
unusual ways. I have known one or two Christians who, in
seeking God's will for their own lives or for the life of their
local church, have in prayer (or, like Abraham, in sleep)
been brought by God into an experience of intense
internal suffering. It has been almost an anticipation in
one person's inner spirit of suffering by the people of God.
At such times God seems to be sharing, temporarily and
traumatically, a small part of his own suffering.

I think I learn one further lesson from this striking
incident in Abraham's life of faith. We should, perhaps, be
more reticent in pushing God for too many details about
the future in our desire to have greater assurance about his
will – unless we are also prepared to enter more fully into
the fellowship of his sufferings 'for the sake of his body,
the church' (see Col. 1:24; Phil. 3:10). At the same time we
can see that God somehow gathers up Abraham's doubts
and his hesitant faith into an expanding revelation of his
purpose for his friend's life, family and future. It is God
who takes Abraham into this salutary experience of
suffering: Abraham does not initiate it.

We must also reject immediately any suggestion that the Lord was making Abraham pay for his doubts with an unpleasant experience. This much is plain from the timing of this deep sleep; it came after he had prepared the animals, which were necessary for the ritual of the covenant, but before God actually entered into the covenant. So God's last word to Abraham was the promise of the covenant, not a prophecy of suffering. God does not leave his friends teetering on the brink of threatened disaster. His last word to us is always of covenant love and faithfulness. However much we are called to share the sufferings of Christ for the sake of his body, the church, we rest in the eternal security of the new covenant in Christ's blood. (See Col. 1:20-3 as a vital prelude to 1:24; cf. Heb. 13:20,21.) That is God's last word to us, dramatically encapsulated in Christ's own last word on the Cross: 'It is finished' (John 19:30). That is the ultimate answer to the question, 'How am I to know that I shall possess the land?' or any other question about assurance posed by any descendant of Abraham. Whatever we are called to go through, we have the promise of the Lord, splendidly captured in the hymn 'How Firm a Foundation', especially:

> The soul that on Jesus has leaned for repose
> I never will leave or desert to its foes:
> That soul, though all hell should endeavour to shake,
> I'll never, no, never, no, never forsake.

7 FORCING THE PACE

Ten years seems a long time to wait for anything. It is now nearly nine years since I moved out of the kind of pastoral and teaching ministry I love. That was in response to a clear call from God to another pattern of ministry in which certain gifts would have to go into cold storage and others hopefully uncovered. During the past nine years I have longed to return to what I left behind in 1976. Often I have asked, or rather urged, the Lord to get on with it. I have sometimes been on the verge of trying to force his hand, doing things my way and in my time. I know in my better moments that God has promised to restore the kind of ministry I find most fulfilling, but it is not easy to hold on to the promise.

I have seen many Christians wrestling with similar situations. God has made clear to them, in ways carefully geared to the personal characteristics of each individual, that in his own time he *will* meet the desires of their hearts – perhaps for a marriage partner, for the gift of a child, for a distinctive sphere of ministry, for a special gift of the Spirit. The promise was definite, but the wait has seemed endless.

The events in Abraham's life since God brought him from Haran to Canaan – the events described so far in the story behind this book – had taken ten long years (Gen. 16:3). In terms of actual fulfilment of God's original promise, nothing much had happened. The promise had been reiterated several times. New details had come to light, firming up the promise and narrowing down the options. Most recently of all, God had entered into a solemn covenant with Abraham. In the light of what had not happened, however, Abraham must have been fairly vulnerable to despair and frustration.

George MacDonald, the Scottish writer of the last century who so greatly influenced C. S. Lewis, wrote: 'That man is perfect in faith who can come to God in the utter dearth of his feelings and desires, without a glow or an aspiration, with the weight of low thoughts, failures, neglects, and wandering forgetfulness, and say to him, "Thou art my refuge."'

A DANGEROUS MOMENT

This was, in other words, a dangerous moment in Abraham's living by faith in God. And trouble did break out – yet not from the direction we might have expected. It came from his wife Sarah. Since the ignominious events in Egypt, Sarah has been notable by her absence from the narrative. It is impossible to know what wounds had been left deep within her as a result of her experience in Pharaoh's harem. Quite possibly she had been more seriously hurt by Abraham's complete self-centredness and insensitivity to her, than by anything that had happened in Pharaoh's palace.

I can think of the long-term impact on a woman whose husband was unfaithful to her. Not only was her faith in God shaken, but inevitably her self-respect and confidence as a person were undermined. Long after the relationship with her husband had been workably restored, it became apparent that she was – unconsciously – turning the children against their father. In addition, it was noticeable that her relationship with the Lord – previously open, joyful, and trusting – now carried overtones of resentment and doubt. Deep down she seemed to blame God for the unfaithfulness and selfishness of her husband. She felt that, above everything else, God had let her down.

I detect a similar attitude in Sarah's comments after these ten barren years. The Genesis narrative has

implicitly made her infertility the chief explanation for
their childlessness. Judging from Abraham's treatment of
his wife in Egypt, he was not the most sympathetic of
husbands. It is not hard to imagine the odd domestic
quarrel, during which Sarah might well have complained
bitterly about all the upheavals and uncertainties caused
by Abraham's mad-cap ideas about God and Canaan.
Abraham's reaction, if in character, might well have
included a callous taunt or reproach about her barrenness.

In such subtle and imperceptible ways family faith is
eroded, to the point where the desire to keep the Lord
central and to do things his way has long been lost. Sarah's
comment to Abraham reflects this: 'Behold now, the Lord
has prevented me from bearing children' (Gen. 16:2).
However close to the truth her remark might have been,
the tone was resentful and the language rebellious. The
couple were not united in spirit – a fact which becomes
unambiguous once events had got out of control: she sees
herself and Abraham as competitors, not companions, as
she calls on the Lord to show on whose side the cause of
justice now lies ('May the Lord judge between you and
me') (Gen. 16:5).

THE MENACE OF SELF-PITY

The Lord had not, in fact, 'prevented' Sarah from having
children. He had postponed the happy event in order to
achieve a far more significant purpose than one woman's
motherhood. Sarah's resentment, and consequently lethal
potential for undermining the faith of her marriage
partnership, stemmed from her preoccupation with her
own desires. Often we inhibit ourselves, as well as those
closest to us, from persevering in faith because we lose
sight of God's greater purposes for our lives. We allow
ourselves to get locked away in our misfortunes. We do not
give up on the Lord; we interpret his faithfulness and
goodness only in terms of our own happiness and fulfil-

ment. If we do not get what we want, we become sullen, spoiled children instead of mature believers.

When we are in this frame of mind, we can become instruments of a lesser god. The name of the one true God remains on our lips, but we are gradually pointing people away from the Lord by our suggestions and our personal influence. We start off playing the part of devil's advocate, but we end up doing it in real life. God-talk is no guarantee of spiritual authenticity – as Abraham was now painfully to discover.

In her disillusionment Sarah had a bright idea: 'The Lord has prevented me from bearing children; go into my maid; it may be that I shall obtain children by her' (Gen. 16:2). Two mitigating factors need to be mentioned immediately. First, theoretically there was still a loophole in the promises of God to Abraham – the name of his son and heir's mother had not yet been spelt out – this was expressly stated only after another thirteen years (Gen. 17:15ff). Secondly, however unlikely and unacceptable Sarah's proposal appears in the light of later biblical morality and modern Christian orthodoxy, her suggestion was entirely consistent with contemporary ethical standards.

The Code of Hammurabi, an extremely enlightened and highly efficient king of Babylonia, probably between 1850 and 1750 BC (i.e. around the time of Abraham), was in operation throughout Mesopotamia and beyond. Both Abraham and Sarah would presumably have been familiar with the code's provisions. Its main principle was 'The strong shall not injure the weak', and on the basis of this code a social order was set up to safeguard the rights of the individual, backed by the authority of Babylonian gods and the state. The code greatly influenced the civilisation of all Middle East countries.

One of the provisions of the Code of Hammurabi ran as follows: 'If a man marries his wife, and she has not given him children, if that man marries his concubine and brings her into his house, then that concubine shall not rank with his wife.' Another provision stated: 'If a man has married a wife, and she has given her husband a female slave who bears him children, and afterwards that slave ranks herself with her mistress because she has borne children, her mistress shall not sell her for silver.... The concubine shall be fettered and counted among the slaves.'

SURROUNDING PRESSURES

When we study the story of Hagar in the light of these two provisions of the Code of Hammurabi, the nuances become more obvious. Sarah's suggestion to Abraham was in line with the accepted norms of the society in which they lived. As we have seen, these norms were considered extremely enlightened, indeed very advanced for such a period of history. With Abraham aged 85 and Sarah over 75, we can imagine the pressures building up on the couple to do something to make God's promise happen: 'After all, God helps those who help themselves' – as the saying still (erroneously) goes.

The surrounding culture thus began to squeeze the couple into its own mould. If the culture said to you, 'Have children by your maid if you can't have them by your wife,' why not? The idea seemed sensible, compassionate, enlightened, simple, natural. Yes, that must be God's way ... and so began the long trail of God's people trying to achieve his purposes in their own way. Faith goes out of the window; common sense and the wisdom of the world take over. The two are not necessarily always in competition, but in this situation they were mutually exclusive. The prevailing wisdom always needs to be checked out against the revelation of God's ways and will in the Bible. Abraham did not pause to check.

I can think of numerous examples of similar situations in which Christians, at the end of their tether, have received apparently good advice from compassionate, enlightened friends – and even family. The advice has come with a lot of God-talk, as with Sarah. For example, young men with strong homosexual drives tearing them apart have been urged, in the name of God's love, to 'have sex' with a prostitute or sleep with a girlfriend. A committed Christian couple, whose marriage is in real difficulty, are encouraged to get a divorce and start again with other partners.

I have discovered over the years that I need to be extremely chary, both of listening to the advice of even the most trusted friends, and of being too ready to offer advice of my own. We can all be unwitting channels for misleading information and advice. This happens with the best will in the world. No mischief is intended. In fact, the advice is normally offered with the very best of motives. But it is unsanctified by prayer or any clear word from God (see 1 Tim. 4:4,5). The 'Sarah syndrome' is, therefore, not only a matter of blatantly anti-Christian counsel from friends whose commitment to Christ as Lord is question-able: it warns us of the Peter principle – moments after being inspired by God to acknowledge Jesus as the Christ, the Son of the living God, Peter becomes the mouthpiece of Satan in urging Jesus to evade the Cross (Mt. 16:13-23).

One personal experience of this kind I recount with sadness, but it makes the point clear. Back in 1971, when we were very uncertain whether to accept an invitation to move to South Africa, I asked the advice of a senior clergyman from whose ministry I had always received much encouragement. He strongly urged me not to leave England, 'because you will move out of the network and become unknown to those who matter'. I do not recall any other details, but I am sure he must have clothed so bald a statement with a suitable covering of God-talk. For some time I was severely shaken, if not thrown, by his 'advice'. God actually turned it to good effect by making me face up not only to the existence of such an influential network, but to my own susceptibility to its influence. Once he had dealt with me at that level, I could look back on the incident with sorrow rather than sourness.

UNHELPFUL ADVICE

A good test to apply to any advice we receive, whether we ask for it or whether it comes gratuitously, is this: does it encourage me to move forward in faith, or does it appeal rather to my natural desires for the security of the familiar, the esteem of others, and the satisfaction of creature comforts? Sarah's advice signally failed such a test. If Abraham had paused long enough to weigh her suggestion against God's revealed word, he would soon have recognised its origin.

But 'Abram hearkened to the voice of Sarai' (Gen. 16:2). After all that the Lord had said to him, he listened to Sarah. God had spoken to Abraham frequently – at least nine times since Ur of the Chaldees. He had spoken clearly – there was no way in which Abraham could have missed the point of what God was saying. He had spoken consistently – over ten long years, the same message, never contradicting himself or going back on his promise. He had spoken personally to Abraham, calling him by name, person to person. He had spoken specifically – specific issues, giving specific promises with specific details.

Abraham had all this clear testimony from the Lord himself; but at the crunch he 'hearkened to the voice of Sarai'. Living by faith means, fundamentally and fearlessly, listening to the voice of God. We can hear God's Word preached week by week; we can study it day by day, in some depth; we can pack it into our heads and pass it on to others; but when the chips are down, we so easily listen to the voice of Sarai, who speaks God-talk and is on our side, but still is the spokesman of Satan. Are we prepared today to listen to the God who speaks to us, and who speaks frequently, clearly, consistently, personally, and specifically?

What was the effect of Abraham taking Sarah's advice to hurry God's programme along? If we were to listen too carefully to certain plausible voices today, we would assume that it obviously didn't work out because God was not in it. The opposite is true: there were immediate results – 'Abram went into Hagar and she conceived. . . . Hagar bore Abram a son' (Gen. 16:4–15). That is the nub of the problem about doing God's work in our own strength: there will be results; there will be success, by many people's yardstick. A son is born to Abraham; the plan has worked. Because it has worked, it must surely be from God – or so many would have us believe in parallel situations today. The Christian church is littered with 'successful' ventures with God's name attached to them which were conceived and brought to birth with human ingenuity and worldly resources. It is amazing what a strong personality, a conducive climate and strong financial backing can achieve. It takes a brave man to stand up and call such successful activity 'the works of the flesh'. Yet that is precisely what Ishmael and his future were.

LONG-TERM CONSEQUENCES

We see the solemn seriousness of this when we pause just a moment to register the fact that Abraham's 'success' with Hagar initiated a bitter feud, which has fuelled what is arguably the single most volatile flashpoint in the world today, as the physical descendants of Abraham through Hagar and Sarah perpetuate the Arab-Israeli conflict. As James wrote, referring to that 'little member', the tongue, 'How great a forest is set ablaze by a small fire!' (James 3:5).

Sarah's tongue was a fire, igniting the embers of Abraham's frustration and impatience. His faith became obliterated, at least temporarily, by the calls of his lower nature, what Paul calls 'the flesh'. Paul's classic exposition of the war between the flesh and the Spirit (Gal. 5:16–26) follows on immediately from his explanation of the priority of faith in Abraham, and in all men and women of faith who are sons and daughters of Abraham (Gal. 3:7).

We will return later to Paul's teaching in Galatians

when we return to the sequel of the Ishmael saga. At present, we note that Paul's catalogue of 'the works of the flesh' exactly describes the aftermath of the Hagar tragedy – anger, selfishness, dissension, envy, enmity, strife, jealousy, immorality and impurity (Gal. 5:19,20). We see precisely these things in the family of Abraham from this point onwards. There is scarcely a trace of what Paul calls 'the fruit of the Spirit' – love, joy, peace, patience, gentleness, goodness, faithfulness, meekness, (Gal. 5:22,23). As far as Hagar and Ishmael are concerned, the trail is clear and it does not include any of these things.

The case is clear, I believe, for God's verdict on any attempt to impose our ideas, strengths, or timetable on his purposes. In view of the solemn seriousness of this verdict, I find it strangely moving to see how God retains and demonstrates a tender care for Hagar (Gen. 16:7-14). The very choice of Ishmael as God's name for her son is eloquent: it means 'God hears'. The word 'hear', both in Hebrew and in Greek, is full of meaning. It includes the sense not just of hearing, but of listening carefully, absorbing and taking action. God heard Hagar in this rich and positive sense, even though the essence of her situation lay in the non-faith of Abraham and Sarah.

In the experience of Hagar there is a parable of the way the Lord, in his patient love, deals with the results of our non-faith. The message about the awesome seriousness of doing God's work could be crushing but for the grace of God shown to Hagar. God does not abandon us to our self-willed devices; he remembers how fragile we are as mere mortals. He appreciates the challenge and the cost of living by faith. He urges us to stop and think, rather as Hagar was confronted by the angel with the question, 'Where have you come from and where are you going?'

If we are conscious of having strayed from the narrow path of living by faith, the Lord is putting the same question to us. We need to recall God's original call, the way he has faithfully led us, and the purpose for which he has laid hold of us. He can make good come out of what has been fruitless and empty. There have been few more rewarding experiences in my own pastoral ministry than seeing Christians, driven and disillusioned for years, recapture joy and peace in believing the Lord for fresh springs of living water.

8   RECOVERING CONFIDENCE

Abraham remained in lonely disillusionment, it seems, for thirteen or fourteen long years. That is the likely force of the narrative at the end of the story recounting the birth of Ishmael – 'Abram was 86 years old when Hagar bore Ishmael to Abram. When Abram was 99 years old the Lord appeared to him' (Gen. 16:16;17:1). The next two chapters gradually unfold Abram's restoration to joy and peace in believing. His friendship with the Lord is back in place, renewed and expectant. There is a sense that the years of waiting are nearly over, that the promise of God is about to be fulfilled. The winter is past, spring is in the air.

There are few Christians who do not experience this winter of the spirit – not necessarily in the aftermath of some Ishmaelite incident, although similar behaviour will easily lead to it. At the time, protracted and claustrophobic as it is, we think that we will never again feel the warmth of God's love in our frozen souls. We wonder whether there is any life left beneath the frosted exterior of our fragile spirituality. God seems to have gone into hibernation or migrated to warmer climes, leaving us to fend for ourselves, exposed and doomed. We struggle along with the residue of hoarded supplies, and with the memories and photographs of summer long past. Will it ever end? Perhaps the unkindest cut of all is administered (however unconsciously) by those privileged to spend all or part of our spiritual winter in the warm sun of God's assured presence: why them and not me, Lord?

'If I had not made that disastrous mistake with Hagar and Ishmael, I would probably not be where I am now.' The sheer loneliness of the winter in our souls seems to accentuate the piercing accusations of our restless consciences. We go round and round, down and down, on the vicious spiral of self-analysis. The 'if only's' mount up remorselessly, and it no longer seems possible to regain perspective and poise.

A NEW NAME

But the Lord did appear to Abraham, disclosing himself by a new and magnificent name – in the Hebrew, El Shaddai, God Almighty, the God who is enough, the God who suffices. It is difficult not to see in this self-revelation a direct but gracious riposte to Abraham's attempt to help God's purposes along with his own ideas and resources. 'I do not need your help in that way,' God seems to be saying; 'nor do you need to listen to the advice of Sarah or draw on the wisdom of your contemporaries. Your responsibility is to walk before me, and be blameless.'

The name 'El Shaddai' is used at several key points in the biblical record. It is always reserved for situations of desperate need, if not completely impossible situations. It comes regularly, and significantly, in the book of Job. There, this distinctive name of the Lord is on the lips of three of Job's four friends, on Job's own lips, and eventually, when he was allowed to speak, on the Lord's own lips. (See, for example, Job 5: 17 – Eliphaz; 8:3 – Bildad; 32:8 – Elihu; 6:4,12:3,21:15,27:2 – Job; 40:2 – God.) The frequent occurrence of the name indicates that the phrase had become, rather like many of us today when we recite the Creed ('I believe in God, the Father Almighty'), almost meaningless for people like Job and his friends. It needed to be rediscovered as a glorious description of God's complete adequacy for even the most impossible situation.

On two important occasions in the life of Jacob, Abraham's grandson, God as El Shaddai is mentioned: by his father Isaac immediately after Rebekah had persuaded

him that he must leave home to escape the vengeance of
Esau; secondly, when God himself speaks to Jacob much
later, after his return to Canaan and reconciliation with
Esau, and promises to give the land to him and his
descendants in accordance with his covenant with
Abraham (Gen. 28:3;35:11).

This particular name, therefore, is very much linked
with God's reiteration of his covenant with Abraham. As
we trace the details of this springtime in Abraham's walk
before God, we see immediately that God is forcing him
back to the covenant originally made with the ritual of the
slaughtered animals before the birth of Ishmael. Thus the
Lord is telling Abraham: 'We are friends – whatever may
have happened in the past, I'm your friend, and you are my
friend.' Repeatedly God stresses the covenant: 'I will make
my covenant between me and you.... Behold, my
covenant is with you.... I will establish my covenant
between me and you and your descendants after you
throughout their generations for an everlasting covenant'
(Gen. 17:2,4,7).

THE JOB OF RESTORATION

Abraham was overwhelmed with relief and gratitude – 'he
fell on his face' (Gen. 17:3) – an act of adoration not
hitherto recorded in the story. There is a special loveliness
in the new joy of someone restored to God's peace after
years of silence and emptiness. The Lord sees himself to be
overjoyed to have his friend back where he belongs. In
reiterating the original promise, behind the covenant, he
adds a number of extra details. Two stand out: the use of
the word 'everlasting' to describe both the covenant and
the family's possession of the land (Gen. 17:7,8); and the
re-naming of Abram as Abraham, stressing the sheer
number of descendants which he was to receive (Gen.
17:5).

The Lord wants Abraham to be in no doubt that
nothing has changed between them, that God holds

nothing against him, and that the future is sure. It is difficult not to sense the air of expectancy in the conversation – but there are still some matters to be faced, three to be precise, and they follow in sequence in the rest of chapter 17 and the first part of chapter 18.

The first event is God's insistence on the rite of circumcision as a mark of the covenant between God and Abraham: 'Every male among you shall be circumcised. . . . So shall my covenant be in your flesh an everlasting covenant' (Gen. 17:10,13). The movement of the narrative and the sequence of events both indicate that this new development is, in God's mind, linked with Abraham's independent assertion of his will over Hagar and Ishmael. In spite of the solemnity and finality of the original covenant ceremony, Abraham had gone his own way. He had treated his friendship with God flippantly.

God, therefore, wanted Abraham – and his future family – to have an unmistakable and unmissable reminder of this covenant. That meant something physical. Because the covenant was bound up with the procreation of children, the male sexual organ was the obvious place. The independence of Abraham had been expressed in a sexual way – it would now be difficult for him to repeat his behaviour without being forcefully reminded of his covenant friendship with the Lord, both its promises and its implications.

Circumcision did not *make* Abraham a friend of God: it indicated that he *was* a friend of God. Abraham did not think up the idea of circumcision: God enjoined it on him and his family. The covenant stood long before the rite of circumcision; in this important sense, circumcision is not essential to the covenant, only subsidiary. Circumcision was intended to remind Abraham of God's covenant, not to prod God's memory about their friendship. Circumcision was, from the beginning, not restricted to Abraham's male descendants; it was necessary for any males bought from another to serve in his family-home. So, from the outset, God clearly had in mind, as a people

for his own possession, a family not restricted to the purely
physical offspring of Abraham.

A DAILY REMINDER

Circumcision, then, was at one and the same time both a
gift of grace on God's part and an act of obedience on
Abraham's part. From both perspectives it focused on the
friendship between them. God realised – and Abraham
must have readily acknowledged – that such a physical
reminder on a daily basis was essential if a mortal man was
going to maintain their friendship through consistent
living by faith. It is a testimony to Abraham's obedience
that 'that very day Abraham and his son Ishmael were
circumcised, and all of the men of his house were
circumcised with him' (Gen. 17:26,27). Of course, as the
steady drift of history was to demonstrate, no outward or
physical sign could guarantee the continuous exercise of
faith in Abraham, or in any of his descendants, natural or
spiritual: 'True circumcision is not something external
and physical. . . . Real circumcision is a matter of the heart,
spiritual and not literal' (Rom. 2:28,29).

But in spite of the limitations of circumcision, or of any
outward sign, in the life of faith, we would be most unwise
to dismiss the importance of such visual aids, not least
because they are God's gifts to us to underline his
faithfulness and our vulnerability. Abraham's circumcision had the further effect of assuring him that any
impact of his disobedience and faithlessness in the matter
of Hagar and Ishmael had been eradicated. Paul's way of
stressing this is to underline Abraham's righteousness, or
the freedom of a right relationship with God, before he
was circumcised – 'he received circumcision as a sign or
seal of the righteousness which he had by faith while he
was still uncircumcised' (Rom. 4:11). Every day – in bed
inside the tent with Sarah or relieving himself outside the
tent – Abraham could remind himself that God had

forgiven and forgotten: El Shaddai is my friend. The Lord is sufficient. With him I have enough, more than enough.

The Christian gospel has long since removed the necessity for circumcision amongst Abraham's spiritual descendants, 'for in Christ Jesus neither circumcision nor uncircumcision is of any avail, but faith working through love.... Neither circumcision counts for anything, nor uncircumcision, but a new creation' (Gal. 5:6;6:15). Paul radically re-interprets the meaning of circumcision for God's people when he describes the crucifixion of Jesus as a circumcision. What was cut off then was not part of 'the flesh of his foreskin', but 'the body of flesh' with all the sins and trespasses attached to it – not, of course, Christ's own sins, but the sin of the world (see Col. 2:11-14).

In this way, God brought about full reconciliation with those who lived completely independently of his will. The whole self-assertive principle was excised in the death and resurrection of Jesus. Baptism dramatically celebrates this radical, total and inward circumcision of 'the flesh' which Jesus experienced for us. This inner transformation, which Paul calls 'a new creation' launches us into a life of 'faith working through love'. Baptism can be, therefore, as powerful a seal of God's covenant love for us as circumcision was for Abraham. Sharing in the Lord's Supper is an equally powerful sacrament, sign and seal of what God has done in making us his friends through Jesus. We are foolish to ignore the value of either visual aid, since both (like circumcision for Abraham) are gifts of grace and acts of obedience.

I HAVE BEEN BAPTISED.

Martin Luther was constantly assailed by vicious temptations from Satan as 'the accuser of the brethren'. He had particularly vivid impressions of the devil lurking in the corner of his study, goading him with accusations of his sinfulness, failures and unacceptability before God.

Apparently, Luther flung his ink-pot across the room and exclaimed: '*Baptismatus sum* – I have been baptised!'

When the tempter gets to work today, it is often wise to make proper use of these two means of grace provided by the Lord. Renewing our baptismal vows (not, I believe, repeating our baptism, but perhaps with water available for symbolic purposes), and regular participation in holy communion with direct application to specific tempt-ations, experiences and needs: these, when practised with faith in the living God, are extremely valuable.

Living by faith does not, therefore, involve any light dismissal of external means of grace. We all need reminders, signs, and visual aids. God knows that we need them and he has provided them. Water, bread, and wine – apart from any other significance in the two sacraments of the Gospel – are ordinary, everyday things. Only a proud person will look down on such means of grace in God's daily gifts. The Christian in touch with his own frailty will acknowledge the realistic generosity of God in thus instituting practical support for living by faith.

THE PLACE OF ISHMAEL

The second hard reality in Abraham's life is the presence and place of Ishmael in his affections, or rather his ambitions. Ishmael represented the daily, visible evidence of his faithlessness. At the age of 13, and with no sign of any other son on the way or remotely likely to be born to a couple in their nineties, Ishmael represented to Abraham the only tangible hope of an heir to inherit God's promise. We must remind ourselves that God and Abraham had never discussed the matter of Ishmael – certainly not before Abraham went into Hagar, and apparently at no stage since then. However much he might have guessed God's reaction by instinct, Abraham did not know what God truly felt about the whole string of events, let alone his plans – if any – for Ishmael.

When we go ahead with our own schemes and rely on our own strength, there will never be any assurance about God's blessing and favour. We will always have that uncomfortable feeling that we are not in the pathway of God's will. Different people react differently to such uncertainty. Some bluff it out with excessive bravado, insisting loudly that God has led them and is with them in their efforts. Others will put a calm face on things and plug on with resignation. One or two tend to lose hope completely and virtually throw in the towel because they realise they have, through their own wilfulness, chosen the wrong road.

Abraham still nursed the hope that Ishmael might turn out to be God's choice. Until we see the seriousness of doing God's work in our own strength, we also will be reluctant to admit that God must discard our self-motivated achievements. The longer things continued unchanged, the older he and Sarah grew, the more desperate he became to vindicate his behaviour and to have Ishmael accepted by God. Thus, when God says explicitly that his heir will be a son born to Sarah, the mixture of unbelief and pride in Abraham flares up and implores God: 'O that Ishmael might live in thy sight!' (Gen. 17:18).

Abraham is saying to God, 'Lord, bless my way of doing things. I can't take in this business of a transcendent God who works miracles in human lives – that is too big, too remote for me. But I have got a son, Ishmael. Let's be reasonable, Lord – use him. Bless my work, my efforts, bless me and my achievements.'

GOD'S STRAIGHT ANSWER

And God says, 'No' (Gen. 17:19). Unequivocally, summarily, finally, 'No.' We do not like anyone saying 'No' to us, especially when it flies in the face of our deepest desires. It is particularly painful when God says 'No' to our ambitions and wishes. It hurts because our pride is rudely

shattered – even if, like Abraham, we have known all along
that God would, once we allowed him close enough to
engage us in conversation, say a very clear and firm 'No'.

I can think of a young divorcee, with a child by another
man, recently converted to a vibrant faith in the Lord.
Living on her own with her child, she often felt the
stabbing pangs of loneliness. It was not surprising when
she explained that a man was paying her a lot of loving
and kind attention. But he was not a Christian, and her
new-found faith told her from the outset that there could
be no future in the relationship. She kept it going,
guardedly but hoping against hope, and found herself
getting into more and more confusion and unhappiness.
When she eventually came honestly to God about the
relationship, she knew he was saying 'No.' After a painful
tussle, she accepted God's word to her.

God's 'No' is always very difficult to accept. But if we
want to know the fullness of God's blessing in our lives; if
we want to enter into all that he has planned for us; if we
want to develop our God-given potential to the full; then
we have to let Ishmael go – to say goodbye to our way of
doing things, our work, our efforts. God says 'No' to all
kinds of Ishmaels in our lives because they have not been
the fruit of his Spirit's instigation and power. Because they
come from our own hearts, they lock us up within the
limits of our own resources. Abraham could not bring
himself to believe in God for the gift of Isaac, because he
was bound to Ishmael. He could not have Isaac and
Ishmael together – the one had to go. We also cannot move
forward into what God has for us until we accept that God
says 'No' to our Ishmaels.

The tragedy of so many Christians is that we stick
within the limits of what we can cope with. If that is where
we want to remain, God will not force us to move against
our will, to move onward and forward. If we want to see
and to know more of God, God will increase our faith, and
we will see more. God is inviting us to come into
uncharted (by us) territory: 'Is anything too hard for the

Lord?' (Gen. 18:14). To repeat, we may stay where we are. Our lives may well be useful, but we will miss God's best for us. There will be good things, but the good is so often the enemy of the best.

This principle seems to stand out clearly in God's decisions about Ishmael and Isaac respectively – 'I will bless Ishmael, but I will establish my covenant with Isaac' (Gen. 17:21). God did not abandon Ishmael, but his purposes were enshrined in Isaac. This is stated in New Testament terms by Paul when he urges every Christian to take care how he builds on the foundation of Jesus Christ:

> Now if anyone builds on the foundation with gold, silver, precious stones, wood, hay, straw – each man's work will become manifest: for the Day will disclose it, because it will be revealed with fire, and the fire will test what sort of work each one has done. If the work which any man has built on the foundation survives, he will receive a reward. If any man's work is burned up, he will suffer loss, though he himself will be saved, but only as through fire (1 Cor. 3:12–15).

If we are not prepared to move on with God from the point where we are now, and to keep on moving with him, then our Christian lives will be Ishmaelite, and they will be burned up in terms of eternal significance. If, on the other hand, we are prepared, however hesitantly and half-heartedly, to accept God's 'No' and to launch out with him, the faith will come and will grow. He will see to that.

THE PROBLEM OF SARAH

The final issue God proceeded to tackle in Abraham's life was Sarah herself. She had a chequered past and God in his love wiped it out with a stroke and gave her a new name: 'You shall not call her Sarai, but Sarah shall be her name' – and he adds for good measure, 'and I will bless her' (Gen.

17:15,16). It seems unclear what the change in name specifically signified, but the change in her future situation is what mattered – she would be a mother: for Sarah there could have been no greater indication of the Lord's blessing. And then suddenly there came to Abraham the news the couple had hoped, with increasing desperation over twenty-five years, to hear: 'I will establish my covenant with Isaac, whom Sarah shall bear to you at this season next year' (Gen. 17:21).

'Next year' – the first indication of a specific date. Abraham now had something definite on which to base his future. We do not know how much he told Sarah in the next few days and weeks. It seems likely that he did not say a word, because Sarah was completely staggered when she overheard the news later. The Lord came – in somewhat unrecognisable fashion – to speak with his friend Abraham, 'as he sat at the door of his tent in the heat of the day' (Gen. 18:1). After some initial comings and goings, the Lord spoke directly to him: 'I will surely return to you in the spring, and Sarah your wife shall have a son' (Gen. 18:10).

Listening to the conversation just inside the tent, Sarah could not suppress a hollow laugh: 'It had ceased to be with Sarah after the manner of women' (Gen. 18:11) is the quaint, but devastatingly appropriate, comment of the narrator. Sarah was completely sceptical about God's promise and his ability to implement it. She simply did not believe it could happen. When the Lord chided her for her unbelief, she was properly afraid, and the Lord left it there. Abraham had himself laughed when God had first promised him a son through Sarah (Gen. 17:17). There was probably the same kind of unbelief in his heart as there was a bit later in Sarah's. 'Our complaint often is not that God gives so little, but that he offers too much.'[1]

God had nothing much more to say to them both. He had brought their hidden unbelief to the surface and forced them to face up to it. He had spoken his definite word of promise into their unbelief. The moment of truth was round the corner. So he left them with the rhetorical question to end all rhetorical questions: 'Is anything too hard for the Lord?' Faith is inextricably linked with our attitude to that question. It is easy to treat it intellectually as rhetorical – a question which needs no answer, because the answer is obvious to anyone. But our minds say one thing, and our inner hearts are drawing up a list of the things which we find too hard for God.

When this inner conflict becomes too painful to bear, it is a huge relief to realise that ultimately God is in control and he is keeping to his predetermined schedule: 'At the appointed time I will return to you, in the spring, and Sarah will have a son.' The last twenty-five years had not been haphazard or pointless. Abraham and Sarah had not destroyed, or even damaged, God's purposes by their doubts, fears and unbelief. God had been weaving everything into his premeditated pattern. Living by faith means such a ready, but not an irresponsible, acceptance of God's sovereignty.

9   SHARING GOD'S HEART

God has cleared away three important obstacles blocking the progress of his friendship with Abraham. We now come to the famous, and frightening, story of Sodom and Gomorrah. It gives us many fascinating insights into the friendship between God and Abraham (Gen. 18:16–19:38). It is important to read the account carefully and thoroughly. As we do so, we must recall Lot's decision, at least twenty-five years previously, to live in Sodom, in spite of the fact that the wickedness of the city was already notorious (Gen. 13:10–13). We remember also that Bera, the king of Sodom, had encountered Abraham after the city's possessions had been recaptured from their enemies. That encounter had left the king of Sodom in little doubt about the moral standards required by 'the Lord God Most High, maker of heaven and earth' (Gen. 14:17–24).

More than a generation had passed, therefore, in which the people of Sodom had persisted in corrupt and wicked behaviour. Because the name 'Sodom' has come into the English language as the archetype of aggressively unashamed homosexual practices, we need to do a bit of biblical homework to establish more precisely the nature of Sodom's wickedness.

SODOM'S MANY SINS

When Ezekiel, over a thousand years later, exposes the unfaithfulness of Jerusalem, he talks of its behaviour as 'the deeds of a brazen harlot' (Ezek. 16:30), actually far worse than the wickedness of Sodom. Ezekiel then describes the state of Sodom in Abraham's time: 'Behold, this was the guilt of your sister Sodom. She and her daughters had pride, surfeit of food, and prosperous ease, but did not aid the poor and needy. They were haughty, and did abominable things before me, says the Lord God; therefore I removed them when I saw it' (Ezek. 16:49,50). This immediately puts into perspective the homosexuality of Sodom; it went hand-in-hand with a blatantly self-indulgent lifestyle and callous indifference to those in need. Surrounding all this was a haughty pride which refused to listen to any reproof and actually gloried in its shame. In the light of these factors, it is not surprising to read also that 'they gave themselves up to sexual immorality and perversion' (Jude 7).

Against this general backcloth the specific actions of the men of Sodom, 'both young and old' (Gen. 19:4), on the night before the city was destroyed, take on an intelligible appearance. Their behaviour was consistent with the overall lifestyle of the city at the time. We read that they surrounded Lot's house when they knew he had visitors, and demanded 'Where are the men who came to you tonight? Bring them out to us, that we may know them.' There was a nasty whiff of angry violence in the air. 'Lot went out of the door to them, shut the door after him, and said, "I beg you, my brothers, do not act so wickedly. Behold, I have two daughters who have not known man; let me bring them out to you, and do to them as you please; only do nothing to these men, for they have come under the shelter of my roof"'(Gen. 19:4–8).

Had it not been for the intervention of the two guests in Lot's house, who – fortunately for him – turned out to be angels, Lot would have been murdered: 'Then they pressed hard against the man Lot, and drew near to break the door. But the men put forth their hands and brought Lot into the house to them, and shut the door. And they struck with blindness the men who were at the door of the house, both small and great, so that they wearied themselves groping for the door' (Gen. 19:10,11). Mob rule and violence were the order of the day in Sodom. Such behaviour is ugly and sinister when, for whatever reasons, people take things into their own hands to achieve their ends – whether on picket lines in England, at funeral processions in Ireland, in political-religious demonstrations in India, or with hooligans on the rampage after soccer matches.

MORAL INDIGNATION

There is one further cameo in the Genesis account of events on the last day of Sodom. When Lot remonstrated with the men of the city, their attitude was one of indignation: 'This fellow came to sojourn, and he would play the judge!' (Gen. 19:9). Here was a city full of arrogance – proud and prosperous, with a surfeit of food but totally callous towards the poor and needy, where mob rule was the order of the day, and where violence stalked the streets at night. And in such a city, identical with most modern cities, we find a most amazing phenomenon: when Lot tried to remonstrate with them, they indignantly retorted, 'This fellow came to sojourn, and he would play the judge!'

That is classic and contemporary. People who strongly assert their right to run their own lives without outside interference and to run society in the way they choose, and on that basis work out a pattern of life which they reckon to be right for them – such people, when somebody tells them what they are doing is wrong, become morally indignant. The net impression is that it seems far more morally reprehensible to have moral standards and to keep them, than to blazon abroad the fact that you have no moral standards.

Along with such moral indignation went a totally flippant attitude to divine judgement. 'Lot went out and said to his sons-in-law who were to marry his daughters, "Up, get out of this place, for the Lord is about to destroy

the city." But he seemed to his sons-in-law to be jesting'
(Gen. 19:14). It was a joke! God does not punish! It was a
repeat of men's reactions when they saw Noah building a
boat in his back yard, 300 miles from the sea. Would God
flood the earth? You must be joking! God doesn't do that
kind of thing – flood countries, destroy cities, strike
cathedrals and minsters with fire – how primitive can you
get!

Sodom was in a desperately serious condition. In one
sense, the depth of its wickedness is most clearly visible in
its pervasive impact on Lot and his family. Lot was not an
ungodly man. We know that daily he was tortured by what
went on in Sodom. But its wickedness had contaminated
the whole family. He was ready to sacrifice the virginity –
and much else – of his daughters to prevent something he
thought far worse from happening. His wife had allowed
the Sodomite way of life to take possession of her heart,
and she could not bring herself to say a final farewell to its
pleasures and prosperity (Gen. 19:26). His daughters were
so determined to have children of their own that they
engineered their father into incest (Gen. 19:30–8). When
the time came to leave the doomed city, we read that Lot
lingered and had to be seized by the hand and propelled
out of the city – 'the Lord being merciful to him' (Gen.
19:16).

Every reaction of each member of the family is
completely understandable. But if we are honest, we must
admit that we understand, and even sympathise with, Lot
and his family because we too are contaminated by 'the
fleeting pleasures of sin' (Heb. 11:25). We, too, linger and
dally when we know it is dangerous to do so. We, too, find
it hard to believe that God still takes sin that seriously.

A HARD DECISION

This was the situation which God decided to share with
his friend, Abraham. The messengers, through whom and

in whom the Lord had already made plain the imminent gift of a son to Sarah, were already on their way to investigate the true seriousness of Sodom's wickedness (Gen. 18:16–22). Although the outcry against Sodom and Gomorrah was great and their sin very grave, God still hesitated to destroy them; he would wait till the evidence had been fully collected. But he determined to tell Abraham about it all – not without some inner debate:

> Shall I hide from Abraham what I am about to do, seeing that Abraham shall become a great and mighty nation, and all the nations of the earth shall be blessed by him? No, for I have chosen him, that he may charge his children and his household after him to keep the way of the Lord by doing righteousness and justice: so that the Lord may bring to Abraham what he has promised him (Gen. 18:17–19).

Abraham's friendship with God involved him, therefore, in God's own agony about the wickedness of a city which had given itself over to self-indulgence and arrogant pride. God, as always, took the initiative in involving Abraham in his feelings, desires and purposes. To be a friend of God and to enjoy his friendship necessarily leads to such painful identification with what lies heavy on his heart.

God decided to open his heart to Abraham because he knew that what Abraham learned from the Lord's attitude to the wickedness of Sodom would stand him in good stead in the future. If Abraham was going to become 'a great and mighty nation' which would bring blessing to every nation on earth, he needed to be absolutely clear about the things which make any nation great and mighty – i.e. practising righteousness and justice, beginning in the home and spreading out like ripples into the wider family, the community, the nation, and international affairs.

In this way Abraham would learn that God's specially chosen people were to be 'a holy nation' (see 1 Peter

2:9-12), distinctively different from all other nations and bringing blessing by their distinctiveness. God's decision to share the details of his attitude to Sodom and Gomorrah was, therefore, crucial for our understanding today of the church's role in the world in general, and of the church of one particular country in that nation.

This proper sense of responsibility by the Christian church for the welfare of the nation in which it is placed is very difficult to accept and to fulfil. It is costly and it is dangerous. It requires continual readiness to give ourselves to intercessory prayer. It means taking as our basis and motivation both the gift of salvation through the death and resurrection of Jesus, and the reality of divine judgement – and living, loving, and praying accordingly. Some of the more detailed implications of this will emerge as we continue with the story of Abraham and Sodom. Before we do that, we need to notice two more things.

UNSUCCESSFUL INTERCESSION

First, taking an overall view of the story in Genesis 18 and 19, Abraham's involvement through intercessory prayer in the situation at Sodom was unsuccessful. Sodom was not spared. Even Lot lost his wife. I learn from this that both the purpose and the value of such intercession does not lie in its results or its effectiveness. God called Abraham as his friend into the place of prayer. In prayer God taught Abraham many things which mattered, especially for the future. In prayer Abraham was getting to know God better. Living by faith means learning to appreciate prayer in this way. It is not a matter of claiming great results, so much as entering into the very heart of God. Living by faith, let me repeat, is a gift for all God's friends. It inevitably involves the painful as well as the pleasant experiences of God's life. Are we ready to share God's agony over, for example, the Sodomite (in its full, not its limited, sense) condition of the western world, and the way so much of the Christian church in the west is contaminated by it?

The second point to note is this: God says of the sin of Sodom, 'The outcry has come to me' (Gen. 18:21). That was said to Cain after he had murdered Abel: 'The voice of your brother's blood is crying to me from the ground' (Gen. 4:10). God hears and takes due notice of all human cruelty, injustice, violence, selfishness, pride and wickedness. As far as Sodom was concerned, that cry had been going up to heaven for a long time. God is extremely patient with a nation's sinfulness. He sends many messengers to warn people of his requirements and what will happen if there is no repentance, no change. He does not act arbitrarily or precipitately; he closely investigates what is happening. The pattern is unmistakable with Sodom; it is even clearer in the later history of Israel, it is abundantly plain in the ministry and message of Jesus; it has been demonstrated over and over again in the centuries since Jesus – the years of God's patience and grace, what history terms AD, 'anno domini'.

In other words, since Sodom, God has not altered his attitude to sin, personal or national. It has not changed, moreover, with the gospel of the kingdom proclaimed by Jesus and the apostles. God's patient waiting, frequent warnings, careful investigation only last a certain time, and the moment comes when God cannot withhold his righteous punishment. Jesus said (concerning the inhabitants of a town which hears the gospel but refuses to repent), 'Truly, I say to you, it will be more tolerable on the day of judgement for the land of Sodom and of Gomorrah than for that town' (Mt. 10:15). Similarly, Capernaum – in which Jesus had done so many mighty works – was solemnly told: 'I tell you that it will be more tolerable for the land of Sodom than for you' (Mt. 11:24). What Jesus declared in connection with specific towns and cities, he made plain in general terms: 'in the days of Lot they ate, they drank, they bought, they sold, they planted, they built; but, on the day that Lot went out from

Sodom, fire and brimstone rained from heaven and destroyed them all. So will it be on the day when the Son of Man is revealed' (Luke 17:28-30).

This is the attitude of the Lord himself to such situations. If we do not like it – and who does like it? – we still have to wrestle with it. The best place to do that is in the place of prayer, into which God calls us as his friends, not in the proud isolation of our own minds, where we so often choose to concoct our own theology with an eclectic smattering of a few favourite biblical texts, interpreted in the light of the rather more congenial trends and tenets of contemporary thinking.

If this is the attitude of the Lord in the face of national and personal wickedness, we can feel the force of these words from what has traditionally been regarded as one of the latest books to be written and included in the New Testament canon,[1] 2 Peter: 'If, by turning the cities of Sodom and Gomorrah to ashes, God condemned them to extinction and made them an example to those who were to be ungodly, and if he rescued Lot, greatly distressed by the licentiousness of the wicked ... then the Lord knows how to rescue the godly from trial, and to keep the unrighteous under punishment until the day of judgement, and especially those who indulge in the lust of defiling passion and despise authority' (2 Peter 2:6-9).

CONCERN FOR LOT

We are now in a better position to look more closely at Abraham's time with the Lord in intercession for Sodom: 'Abraham still stood before the Lord.' God has shared with his friend Abraham what is on his mind and heart as a result of the very grave sin of Sodom. Abraham now begins to share with his friend God what is on his heart. In brief, Abraham's heart goes out to Lot. Although Lot is never mentioned by name in his intercession with the Lord, he is central to Abraham's concern – and the Lord is fully aware of the fact. The Genesis narrative makes this plain when, at the finale, we read: 'So it was that, when God destroyed the cities of the valley, God remembered Abraham, and sent Lot out of the midst of the overthrow, when he overthrew the cities in which Lot dwelt' (Gen. 19:29).

Does Abraham's concern for Lot impair, or even destroy, the integrity of his intercession for Sodom? Does it even explain, as some believe, the failure of his intercession in preventing the destruction of Sodom? These and similar considerations betray, it seems to me, a wrong understanding of intercessory prayer.

It is certainly true that, in Exodus 32, we read of Moses pleading with the Lord not to press ahead with his determination to wipe out the 'stiff-necked' Israelites in punishment for their 'Golden Calf' idolatry. 'The Lord repented of the evil which he thought to do to his people' (v.14). The sequel shows only those actually involved in sinning against the Lord as being punished: 'Whoever has sinned against me, him will I blot out of my book' (v.33). The Lord affirms that he will 'visit their sin upon them', and we are told that the people were as a consequence struck with a plague. This unique incident indeed urges us to faithful, urgent intercession on behalf of those who have walked over God's commandments. But we must beware of reading too much into the phrase translated, 'The Lord repented. . . .' We can always come to God on the basis of his promises and his mercy, as did Moses and Abraham. But we must watch any tendency to overplay this aspect of intercession.

It is sometimes taught that through faithful intercession we can influence God, move him to do things which he does not want to do or would not think of doing unless we persuaded him to do so. Perhaps, it is suggested, we can bring him round to our side and our way of seeing things. Even when this is not expressly taught, the strong impression is left that by the right kind of prayer – if we have enough faith – we can get things out of God.

This incident in Abraham's life shows clearly that God

calls us as his friends into fellowship with himself in prayer. There is no emphasis on Abraham bringing God round to his point of view. The story begins with God deciding to share his mind with Abraham, and the emphasis falls on the seriousness of the city's sin, and the call of God for justice and righteousness. Clearly, God must have referred to his intention to bring destruction on Sodom; otherwise, Abraham would not have begun, 'Wilt thou indeed destroy the righteous with the wicked?' (Gen. 18:23).

The conversation that follows indicates the quality and the cornerstone of Abraham's friendship with God. He shows both a reverent awe and a confident boldness in speaking from his heart to God. He appeals to God's character as a just God, 'the Judge of all the earth' (Gen. 18:25). He senses that his friend is a God of forgiveness and mercy – indeed, he knows it from his own experience. So he is free to ask God to show such forgiveness again (the word 'spare' means 'forgive'). (Gen. 18:24,26). Abraham realises that he is all but presuming on his friendship with God in pressing ahead with his request: 'Behold, I have taken upon myself to speak to the Lord...' (Gen. 18:31). But he presses on, in spite of recognising that he is 'but dust and ashes' (Gen. 18:27).

The story eloquently reveals the intimacy of this friendship. Yet we must allow the details of how the conversation ended to have their full force. Abraham has brought the number of righteous people who might be left in Sodom from fifty down to ten. God says: 'For the sake of ten I will not destroy it.' The narrative then continues, 'And the Lord went his way, when he had finished speaking to Abraham' (Gen. 18:33). The Lord began the conversation; the Lord also ended the conversation. He then proceeded to destroy Sodom, but rescued Lot and his family.

WHY PRAY AT ALL?

We are forced to ask the question: what was the point of Abraham's intercession? If we simply excise the passage which describes God's conversation with Abraham, the narrative follows through without any hiatus. Even the comment that God remembered Abraham and sent Lot out of Sodom before its overthrow can stand as a merciful action on the Lord's part for Abraham's sake – without any intercession on his part for his nephew.

There is, therefore, no necessary causal link between Abraham's intercession and the events surrounding the destruction of Sodom. The three priorities in the incident – from God's perspective – seem to be these: his judgement on sin, his rescue of Lot, and his friendship with Abraham. That conversation between the two friends is important in its own right, not in terms of what is or is not achieved by Abraham's intercession. As a result of what he learned, Abraham understood more of the mind and ways of the Lord. That is why God initiated the conversation; he finished it when Abraham had learned what God wanted to teach him. And God knew the unspoken longing of Abraham's heart that Lot might be spared.

This is not an abstruse pseudo-philosophical discussion about the mysteries of intercessory prayer. God longs for us to spend time with him; that is what a friendship is all about. He wants to hear what is on our minds, and he wants above all to share with us what is in his mind. As we spend quality time together in this way, we become more finely attuned to the will of God. We are then more ready and better equipped to be his witnesses and ambassadors.

The glorious promises about prayer, especially intercessory prayer, in the Scriptures must surely be used in this light. We need to be more sensitive in responding to God's initiative in calling us to prayer, more receptive to what he wants to teach us in prayer, and more immediate in moving from prayer into our daily responsibilities. No doubt all kinds of things will happen, which would not have happened otherwise. But it is quality time spent together as friends that God appreciates, not a semi-mercenary attempt at arm-twisting!

10 REPEATING OUR MISTAKES

'I will return to you in the spring... at this season next year Sarah will bear Isaac'; the time of conception and the virtual date of birth had been announced – by God at any rate. After so many years of waiting for the Lord to fulfil his promise, Abraham must have been full of expectancy and quiet confidence. We expect to see him moving serenely forward in the intervening months before Sarah's conception of a child. God's appointed time was so close.

But living by faith means that no period of time is ever guaranteed to be trouble-free or temptation-free. We often feel we would like a period of plain sailing, when we can simply run with the breeze without any effort or risk – a vacation from the spiritual struggle. Friendship with God is never like that, and Abraham proved strangely vulnerable at a time when he could have pressed forward with joy and hope. He was vulnerable in an area where he had already learned a painful lesson twenty-five years earlier. He repeated the same behaviour at Gerar with Abimelech (Gen. 20:1–18) as he showed in Egypt with Pharaoh.

Abraham, moving to a new home in a strange environment, again tried to pass Sarah off as his sister. The reason, once again, was his fear for his own skin (Gen. 20:11). He showed the same disregard for his wife's honour and dignity – and this was immediately preceding the time when he knew God had promised to ensure Sarah's conception of Isaac. Fear once more eroded Abraham's faith in God.

NO-GO AREAS

Abraham, in fact, revealed a long-hidden weakness in the course of his later conversation with Abimelech, once his foolishness had come to light. We discover that he had forced Sarah into making a bargain with him, long before he actually set foot in Egypt: 'When God caused me to wander from my father's house, I said to her, "This is the kindness you must to do me: at every place to which we come, say of me, He is my brother"' (Gen. 20:13).

So Abraham had, from the beginning, schemed and planned for defeat; he had written a habit of fear and doubt into his future life. So long as this promise was stored away in their relationship, Abraham and Sarah were unable to respond to God with unequivocal faith in many situations. They had, by their decision long ago and by mutual (probably tacit) agreement ever since, turned an important part of their life into a no-go area. After their salutary experience in Egypt, they ought to have thrashed out Abraham's fears in honest discussion. Instead, they found themselves falling into exactly the same trap as before, bringing further damage to their own integrity and further dishonour on the Lord.

I have found it necessary in preparing Christian couples for marriage to discuss no-go areas in their relationship. For example, many couples come to me with their minds already made up about when they are going to have children, how many they are going to have, and even about their intention not to have children at all. However strong the commitment to Christ of such couples, it is rare to find any who have properly consulted the Lord about such fundamental decisions in their life together. Unless their decisions are, at this early stage, questioned and the reasons for them honestly examined, the subject of having children quickly becomes a no-go area. If one or the other later wants to revise the decision in the light of what God seems to be saying, it proves very painful, if not impossible, to raise the subject with any honesty or openness (either with each other or with the Lord).

Most couples have such off-limits territory with each other. Sometimes it has to do with money. Often it revolves around the chores each is expected to do around the house. For some couples there has always been an uneasy truce about personal aversions; they simply do not mention certain topics. Sexual problems are often taboo, as are personal weaknesses like violent temper or neurotic anxiety. We all have such no-go areas, and the underlying reason for them all being so is fear.

Abraham reveals a lot about his true motives in his admission to Abimelech: 'When God caused me to wander from my father's house....' That is a heavily loaded remark, showing little trace of any glad readiness to follow the Lord's guidance. Abraham has also begun to trim down his explicit trust in God in the face of what he perceives to be an unsympathetic audience. I know myself how easy it is to fall into this trap. We do not want to appear too pious, and so we almost excise God from our vocabulary, or at least introduce him rather apologetically. Is that how Abraham would have spoken to the Lord about his call in Haran – 'You caused me to wander from home...'?

God wants to deal with us, gently but firmly, across the board. If we erect barriers across certain parts of our lives, and prohibit others – especially those closest to us – from entering, we will be completely stymied when God wants to bring his grace and truth to bear on them. And he certainly will. As we have already seen, fear is the biggest obstacle to faith. We need, therefore, to receive help from those closest to us in facing up to the situations from which we shrink, not a conspiracy of silence to keep them locked away.

SIN DOES NOT DISAPPEAR

Abraham's repetition of behaviour a quarter of a century

later also warns us about the persistence of human sinfulness. Forgiveness is a glorious reality and is obviously at the heart of the Christian gospel. But even God's forgiveness does not eradicate temptation, let alone make any sin unrepeatable. This is powerfully emphasised by the fact that Abraham travelled the same path, after apparently avoiding it for nearly twenty-five years. We are never too old, experienced, or spiritually mature to regard any sin as finally conquered, or any temptation as unable to affect us.

When Abimelech pressed Abraham to explain why he had passed Sarah off as his sister, Abraham made a significant comment: 'I did it because I thought, There is no fear of God at all in this place, and they will kill me because of my wife' (Gen. 20:11). Abraham behaved as he did because he assumed that Gerar was godless and pagan. He was frightened of the implications of this supposed godlessness for his own safety. Thus fear warped his judgement, eroded his faith and compromised his testimony. The basis for Abraham's conclusions about Gerar lay entirely in his own imagination: what were the facts?

First of all, Abimelech was not an unprincipled and covetous womaniser. As God himself testified, his behaviour towards Sarah had been characterised by complete integrity: 'In the integrity of my heart and the innocence of my hands I have done this' (Gen. 20:5,6). Moreover, Abimelech revealed a far more acute sensitivity to the moral issues at stake than Abraham: 'What have you done to us? And how have I sinned against you, that you have brought on me and my kingdom a great sin? You have done to me things that ought not to be done' (Gen. 20:9). His next question almost has the trenchancy of a prophetic word: 'What were you thinking of, that you did this thing?' (Gen. 20:10). It was this apparently unremarkable question which unlocked Abraham's no-go area with Sarah. If only he had stopped to ask himself that question. . . .

Another impressive aspect of Abimelech's behaviour is his respectful and compassionate treatment of Sarah. He did not rush her into his bed ('now Abimelech had not approached her' – Gen. 20:4) and, after Abraham's duplicity had been uncovered by God, he was determined to preserve Sarah's public reputation amongst their own people and amongst the people of Gerar – 'To Sarah he said, "Behold, I have given your brother a thousand pieces of silver; it is your vindication in the eyes of all who are with you; and before everyone you are righted"' (Gen. 20:16). Abimelech's behaviour towards Sarah stands out in stark contrast with Abraham's. He, the godless king of a godless people in Abraham's mind, showed far greater respect for Sarah as a person and as a woman.

CONCERN FOR SARAH

Abimelech's determination to vindicate Sarah's honour in front of his own people, especially his servants, is also significant. He clearly regarded the moral standards of his employees to be, in very real measure, his solemn responsibility. He did not treat them like dirt; he had regard for their need of self-respect and of maintaining proper standards of decency and mutual support. When God, therefore, made it plain to Abimelech that any failure to restore Sarah to Abraham would bring certain death both to him and his household (Gen. 20:7), he 'rose early in the morning and called all his servants, and told them all these things; and the men were very much afraid' (Gen. 20:8).

We should not let the men's reaction pass without noting that they did not – like the men of Sodom, specially Lot's prospective sons-in-law – mock at the promise of divine judgement on immoral behaviour. They clearly had an in-built sensitivity to the reality both of God's existence and of God's holy requirements. This was consistent with their master's own understanding of God

as a just judge who would not 'slay an innocent people'
(Gen. 20:4).

In summary, then, Gerar was by no means the godless
city which Abraham, in his fear and prejudice, had
concluded. This is, I believe, a fact of great importance
today, when many Christians regard certain areas of
everyday life as irretrievably and utterly corrupt. When my
father, who spent his whole working life in the City of
London at Lloyd's, was introduced to the family of his
fiancee over fifty years ago (my parents have both been
committed Christians from their early teens), he was
regarded with some suspicion by my mother's family
because he was an insurance broker. Two of my brothers
are successful businessmen; they have had a hard time
convincing Christian friends and acquaintances not in the
business world that it may not be completely wicked, that
profit is not necessarily a dirty word, and that people can
live successfully in such a situation without being
ethically compromised.

In fact, the most common complaint about the
preaching ministry of a local church, as brought by
Christians in the world of business, industry, and
commerce, is the way a clergyman tends to regard their
world as nothing but corrupt: 'There is no fear of God at
all in this place.' I have myself been justly corrected for
snide references to 'the rat race'. It is very easy to perpetuate
the myth that God is more at home in the church than in
the world.

There are several destructive results of such a heresy.
Many Christians feel, for example, that they have to opt
out of certain careers because the pressures are seen by
'more mature' Christians as ungodly. Others never
consider taking up such work because they are told it is far
more strategic and uncompromising to be a schoolteacher,
a clergyman, or a doctor. Christians who do move into
commerce, industry, or business feel under suspicion and,
especially as far as their local church is concerned, receive
either no or inadequate encouragement and teaching for

their daily work. For these reasons, and many others, the witness of the Christian church in the regular meeting places of men and women day-by-day is often heavily muted, if not silenced. The modern Abraham stands aloof and complains that there is no fear of God in the city; the modern Lot receives no support and becomes increasingly assimilated into the ways of the city; and the modern Abimelech finds little stimulus for his spiritual quest, and cannot fathom the timid, ambivalent and apologetic behaviour of those known to be men and women of faith.

GOD: PRESENT OR ABSENT?

And what about God? How, in fact, is he involved in such situations? Abraham decided well in advance that God would be noticeable by his absence from Gerar, and acted accordingly. What difference would it have made if Abraham had paused long enough to consult his friend in prayer? From the ending to the Gerar incident it seems that God intended such prayer to be Abraham's major involvement in the affairs of Abimelech and his people (Gen. 20:7-17). Although Abraham seems to have had the wickedness of Sodom embedded in his mind as he came to Gerar, expecting to find much the same there also, he does not appear to have written into his daily life the priority of intercessory prayer.

Abraham was not in tune with the Lord's activity in Gerar. He assumed, out of fear, that Gerar was godless, when in fact God was very much involved in Abimelech's life. Apart from the marks of spiritual hunger and sensitivity already noted, we see that the Lord personally dealt with Abimelech in a very direct way – 'God came to Abimelech in a dream by night' (Gen. 20:3). In other words, God's dealings with the king of Gerar were closely parallel to the way he communicated with his friend Abraham. He spoke specifically and clearly to him in a dream. The Lord also protected Abimelech from being unwittingly led into serious sin: 'It was I who kept you from sinning against me; therefore I did not let you touch Sarah' (Gen. 20:6). He did not hesitate to tell Abimelech what would happen if he snubbed this guardian grace in his life. The way the Lord 'closed all the wombs of the house of Abimelech because of Sarah' can be taken as further evidence of this grace – seen in an evident indication of divine displeasure.

As we draw the threads of this story together, it is clear that Abraham does not come out of it at all well. He did several things which he ought not to have done, and he failed to do the one thing he ought to have done – i.e. consult with God. And yet God did not cast him aside. By this stage we have come to expect such steady faithfulness in the Lord, but we must pause long enough to absorb the wonder of God's grace.

GOD'S INSISTENCE

God was insistent, however, that Abraham take his responsibilities in prayer with full seriousness. In his talk with Abimelech, God says, 'Restore the man's wife; for he is a prophet, and he will pray for you.' When we, also, have failed in living by faith in a given situation, failed in trusting God or bearing clear testimony to his grace, then the way back for us is to the privileged place of intercessory prayer. We are called to hold before God those whose lives we have touched, however inadequately and falteringly. We cannot afford to let fear and failure have the last word; we live by faith when we express our penitence by resolutely picking up once more our privileges as prophets and priests before God.

It is Abimelech, in fact, who a year or so later puts Abraham's unchanging friendship with God in a nutshell. Whilst recognising Abraham's original duplicity and calling for firm guarantees of proper loyalty in the future (Gen. 21:21-34), Abimelech readily acknow-

ledges: 'God is with you in all that you do' (Gen. 21:22).
That is as precise a description of Abraham's friendship
with God as we can find in the Scriptures. The emphasis
falls exactly where Jesus himself placed it in his parting
commission to his friends: 'Lo, I am with you always, to
the close of the age' (Mt. 28:20).

A continuous friendship with the Lord will inevitably
produce in us greater likeness to the Lord – all friendships
have that effect. To that degree, Christians will be very
markedly different from those who do not know the Lord.
But the essential difference is not what we are gradually
becoming, but what we actually are through the grace of
God – i.e. his friends, his sons and daughters. Nothing we
do or fail to do can alter that. Living by faith means
accepting that, and living accordingly.

11 FACING SACRIFICE

'To Abraham and Sarah, at the time when God decided, at home in Gerar. The gift of a son, Isaac. Laugh with us.' It had actually happened, after all those long years of waiting, of faith mixed with doubt, of hope mixed with fear. The narrative repeatedly stresses the faithfulness of God (Gen. 21:1-7) – 'The Lord visited Sarah as he had said, and the Lord did to Sarah as he had promised. And Sarah conceived, and bore Abraham a son in his old age at the time of which God had spoken to him.' Three times in two verses the complete reliability of God's word is under-lined.

In the next few verses, the ready obedience of Abraham is also emphasised. He called his son Isaac; he circumcised the boy when he was eight days old, 'as God had commanded him' (Gen. 21:4). At the age of 100 and 90 respectively, Abraham and Sarah saw their dreams come true. The name Isaac, meaning 'he laughs', which had originally seemed an unnecessary way for God to labour their unbelief and scepticism, now becomes an invitation to celebrate – 'God has made laughter for me; everyone who hears will laugh over me' (Gen. 21:6).

God's promises can often seem a mockery, until we see them fulfilled in our lives. It is very painful to see depressed people struggling with promises of being lifted out of the pit and being given a new song. Many Christians find it virtually impossible, when locked within an apparently intractable illness, to cope with accounts or assurances of God's power to help. I think of a friend with a paralysing fear of flying, forcing herself to make an important journey halfway across the world by repeating the promises of God over and over again.

The agonies of waiting are, however, more than compensated by the joy of fulfilment: 'Who would have said to Abraham that Sarah would suckle children? Yet I have borne him a son in his old age' (Gen. 21:7). We do not know how widely – if at all – Abraham shared his hope of having a child by Sarah. But I have no doubt that, if he did share it, he received no encouragement to believe it could ever happen. Every single human voice would have unanimously said otherwise. Only God gave Abraham any grounds to trust for a son; even Sarah was a dissuader. Sometimes we simply have to press on alone with our faith and our private doubts. God will not let us down. Living by faith is often a lonely existence.

I think, for example, of several Christian couples who have had to watch a child abandon the faith of the parents, perhaps after a time of definite commitment to Christ, and disappear into practical unbelief, often in very wild behaviour. The struggle to hold on in faithful prayer has been extremely intense and costly. I have seen parents go grey with the pain and the strain. They have been held by the promises of God; but it has often been by the skin of their teeth that they have survived a private agony which is very hard to share. But they have survived, by the grace of God, to know the joy of return and reunion.

A NEW CRISIS

It took only a few months for Abraham and Sarah's joy to face its first real test. The arrival of Isaac precipitated a clash and a crisis in the family. Abraham's other son, Ishmael, was now about fourteen. It seems clear that Abraham had naturally lavished great affection on Ishmael. He realised, of course, that God had decided against Ishmael being the one through whom his descendants would fulfil God's destiny for him. Abraham would, however, have been most exceptional if he had not

showered unprecedented love on Isaac. A son of fourteen
would have picked up the implications of such actions;
indeed, his mother Hagar would surely have told him the
whole story by this stage, including his own future as it
had been outlined by the Lord to her (Gen. 16:11,12) and to
Abraham (Gen. 17:20).

The tensions erupted when 'Abraham made a great feast
on the day that Isaac was weaned' (Gen. 21:8). The special
celebrations, the extra attention, the great expectations –
all focused on a baby scarcely able to walk – roused
Ishmael's hot temperament and hidden jealousy: had not
God said he would be 'a wild ass of a man'? (Gen. 16:12).
We read that 'Sarah saw the son of Hagar the Egyptian
laughing at her son, Isaac' (Gen. 21:9). Sarah had invited
everyone to share in her laughter and Ishmael – perhaps he
had heard Sarah's cry of happiness on Isaac's birthday –
decided to join in with the laughter, not in celebration but
in jealous derision.

In the Revised Standard Version we are told that Sarah
saw Ishmael 'playing with her son Isaac'; the Authorised
Version and the Revised Version both use the word
'mocking'. The margin of the Good News Bible has
'making fun of'. Whatever the precise meaning, the
significance of what took place became unambiguous in
Jewish tradition because Paul summed up the situation in
these terms: 'At that time he who was born according to the
flesh persecuted him who was born according to the Spirit'
(Gal. 4:29). 'Isaac, the object of holy laughter, was made
the butt of unholy wit or profane sport.'[1]

In more normal circumstances we would, no doubt,
debate the pros and cons of the alternative courses of
action open to Abraham at this time of conflict. It is not
usually wise to run away from conflict in the family, either
in the local church or in the home. Sarah's reaction to
Ishmael's mockery of Isaac was predictable, in character,
and natural: 'Nobody treats my son like that – Ishmael
must go' (Gen. 21:10). Abraham's protective instincts as
father of both children were also par for the course: 'The

thing was very displeasing to Abraham on account of his son' (Gen. 21:11). Everything paternal welled up in Abraham in reaction against the notion of casting out Hagar and Ishmael – Hagar perhaps, but Ishmael, never.

This was, as we can see, another moment of crisis for Abraham. Left to himself, he would almost certainly have rejected Sarah's demands. But the Lord stepped into the situation with a clear instruction, one which went against the grain for Abraham: 'Be not displeased because of the lad and because of your slave woman; whatever Sarah says to you, do as she tells you, for through Isaac shall your descendants be named' (Gen. 21:12). Abraham was neither accustomed nor inclined to do what his wife told him. The evidence was in the opposite direction. But God told him and Abraham obeyed. Their friendship was by that time so well-established that there was little likelihood of Abraham disobeying God when the message was plain, even when obedience was painful and costly.

UNQUESTIONING OBEDIENCE

Both in this incident with Ishmael and in the dramatic events with Isaac on Mount Moriah several years later (recorded in the following chapter – Gen. 22:1–19), Abraham revealed immediate and unquestioning obedience towards God in the matter of his two sons. With the benefit of hindsight, we can see the advantages which accrued from both decisions. But if we are going to appreciate what living by faith involves, we need to imagine ourselves in each situation.

It is always very difficult to surrender your own children to the will of God, especially to be parted from them – temporarily, let alone permanently. In the case of Ishmael, Abraham was saying goodbye to him for ever. In the case of Isaac, Abraham was expected by God to make an even more radical surrender – not in letting his son physically go, as with Ishmael, but in letting him go emotionally from the very core of his being. In neither case did ultimate events turn out to be as disastrous as Abraham expected: Ishmael was protected, guided and blessed by God; Isaac was not actually sacrificed. But in both cases, the challenge to Abraham's faith came some time before these sequels.

The Mount Moriah incident is prefaced by an intriguing sentence; 'After these things God tested Abraham' (Gen. 22:1). The phrase 'after these things' probably refers to all the previous narrative from the introduction of Abraham into the Genesis narrative. In many ways this story portrays the ultimate challenge faced by God's friend, and it came at the advanced age of well over a hundred. In other words, God tested Abraham in this uniquely searching way, when he could have legitimately thought that he could settle down quietly into a well-earned retirement.

But Abraham remained open to the call of God even after everything he had been through. When God said to him, 'Abraham!' he immediately replied, 'Here I am.' We can appreciate the personal intimacy of Abraham's friendship with God when we note that he responded in exactly the same way, later in this passage, when Isaac called out to him (Gen. 22:7). In other words, his relationship with the Lord was as immediate, close and personal as his relationship with his son. Is our relationship with the Lord like that? In the freedom of such a friendship, Abraham was as ready to go with God as he ever had been in his prime, when he was more footloose and fancy-free.

THE KNIFE WHICH PENETRATES

What exactly was the test which God brought to Abraham? 'Take your son, your only son, Isaac, whom you love, and go to the land of Moriah, and offer him there as a burnt-offering upon one of the mountains of which I shall tell you' (Gen. 22:2). The first ten words in that devastating command are incredibly powerful. They come in four phrases, each of which intensifies the pathos and the drama of what is about to happen. In strictly factual terms, God needed to say only the first three of those ten words: 'Take your son.' That was sufficient to drive a knife into Abraham's heart.

But God goes deeper and deeper into the core of his friend's inner being as he continues, 'Take your son, your only son . . .' – the one you waited for for so long, the child of your old age, the only one left now that Ishmael has gone for ever. 'Take . . . Isaac' – the one who had brought such laughter to your home and restored the joy of being alive, the one who proves how I can do the impossible and that nothing is too hard for me, the one in whom my promises to you will be fulfilled: take Isaac. 'Take Isaac, whom you love . . .' – and love so deeply it almost hurts, who means the world to you and for whom you would gladly lay down your life. 'Take your son, your only son, Isaac, whom you love . ., and offer him as a burnt-offering.'

God asked Abraham for his most treasured possession. What about us? It could be a child (a grown-up child or a young child) whom we have not handed over to the Lord. It could be parents; we may have been married several years, and still not have let our parents go. It could be our husband or our wife, whom we love, but he or she still comes between us and the Lord because we cannot bring ourselves to hand them over. It could be a friend, perhaps the one we want to marry, but we cannot face this test of surrendering the one we love. Invariably, as with Abraham, it is a person who stands between us and the Lord. When Paul wrote to Christians in Galatia, who had started vibrantly living by faith but had been sucked down into an unlively, crippling legalism, his leading question was, 'Who has hindered you?' (Gal. 3:1) – not 'what' but 'who'.

GIVE IT BACK TO ME

God also asked Abraham for what he himself had given him. He wanted Isaac back. That is part, an essential part, of the pain involved in Abraham's response to God. He had waited for so many years for God to give him a son through Sarah. In that son was embodied the fulfilment of God's unique promises. As well as making no sense, God's requirements seemed to attack his very identity as a human being and – even more agonisingly – as a friend of God. How could he face the future if it meant jettisoning all that he had trusted and suffered to gain? Where was the point of God taking away what he had given?

I remember the way this was brought home to my own soul. From the age of nineteen I have asked God to give me the gift of teaching, especially expository teaching of his Word. When I heard Alan Stibbs, whose little book on Abraham I have quoted several times and under whose ministry I was privileged to receive rich insights into the Scriptures, share how at an early age he had asked God for the gift of teaching, I also asked the Lord for it. Through his grace he has given me a deep, passionate love for the Word of God, and even more – in one sense – for expounding it week by week to the congregation of a local church.

After five years of that absorbing kind of ministry in a parish in Cape Town, I was asked to take on a more responsible position, which would inevitably remove me from such an opportunity. I realised that God was wanting to move me on into a situation in which other gifts would be needed. It made no sense whatever to withdraw from a regular teaching ministry. There was hardly anything of that kind in the Anglican Church in South Africa at the time, and a fresh wind of spiritual renewal was blowing strongly through the church; many revitalised Christians required proper grounding in the Scriptures.

The crucial question was put to me by the Archbishop

of Cape Town, who said, 'David, are you prepared to give back to God what he has given to you?' It took a long time to reach the place where I was willing to let God have back what I knew he had given me, and what was really at the heart of my calling as a Christian and even my very personhood.

God often calls us to make similar sacrifices which defy common sense. Abraham's sacrifice defied all logic. Whatever discipline of the mind he might have brought into operation, the whole thing made no sense. I am like many, particularly western, Christians who find it very hard, in practice, to recognise that our minds are not the final arbiter of what God wants. To analyse, diagnose, reach conclusions from an objective standpoint: these activities do not enable us to reach the mind of God, let alone to sum up his mind. God is greater than our minds. He wants us to love him with all our mind, heart, soul and strength. He wants our minds to be totally at his disposal, but we must never let common (or not so common) sense dictate to us what God is saying. Many times he will lead us through common sense; but many times he says to us, 'Common sense says one thing, but I am asking the opposite.'

UNCONSECRATED STRENGTHS

Another aspect of God's call to Abraham to sacrifice Isaac is that he asks us to hand over our strengths. In requiring him to send away Ishmael, God was in effect marking the end of Abraham's self-will, his flesh-controlled decisions, his weaknesses. In the Isaac story, it is a matter of what God had enabled him to be. As Paul put it, in the verse from Galatians already quoted, Ishmael was 'born according to the flesh', while Isaac was 'born according to the Spirit' (Gal. 4:29). Most Christians, however great the struggle, want to be rid of their Ishmaels and of the powerful drives which produce them. Very few find it easy or pleasant to surrender their strengths. It is only when God summons us to come with our *strengths* to Mount Moriah that we begin to appreciate how firmly we hold on to our gifts, instead of trusting in the Giver.

For all these reasons, Abraham's instant obedience to God's call is extremely striking. We will, therefore, find that the details of the narrative provide strong incentive for us to travel the same road when God speaks to us in the same vein. Abraham was living close to the Lord; their relationship brought both clarity and perception into God's will and ready obedience to God's word: 'So Abraham rose early in the morning' (Gen. 22:3). The journey from Beersheba to Moriah took over two days: 'On the third day Abraham lifted up his eyes and saw the place afar off' (Gen. 22:4). Abraham had over forty-eight hours to think over what he was doing. You don't ride an ass for two whole days, and sleep under the stars for two long nights, without mulling over many things, probably your entire life. Abraham had many chances to reconsider and to run away from God.

What kept him pressing forward? 'They went, both of them, together' (Gen. 22:6,8) says the narrative (twice) in its marvellously evocative economy of words. What sustained them? The secret is in a truth about Abraham which became apparent at the beginning of his friendship with God. When they reached their destination, 'Abraham said to his young men, "Stay here with the ass; I and the lad will go yonder and worship"' (Gen. 22:5). Worship was the very heart of Abraham's life. Out of it sprang everything else. If I had been in that situation and had forty-eight hours or more to mull over what was happening, I am sure that something like this would have gone through my mind: 'What have I done? Where have I gone wrong? God is trying to teach me some terrible lesson. I must have done something to have prompted this awful situation. God is punishing me.' These were clearly not the thoughts of Abraham, nor would they be the thoughts of anyone who is assured of the love of God.

A RESURRECTION FAITH

In fact, we read in the gallery of faith in the letter to the
Hebrews that Abraham trusted God because he believed
that God was able to raise men even from the dead (Heb.
11:19). There is actually a hint of this, which we should
not labour, in the closing phrase of his instructions to his
servants: 'I and the lad will go yonder and worship, and
come again to you.' As Paul put it, Abraham believed in
'the God . . . who gives life to the dead' (Rom. 4:17) – and he
had none of the evidence that we have.

From the hallowed ground of worship, with the faith
which that inspired and the friendship with God which
that expressed, Abraham received strength to press firmly
onwards with what God had called him to do. The
pervading theme of the drama is contained in the name
Abraham gave to the place, after God had stopped him on
the brink of killing his son: Jehovah-jireh, 'the Lord will
provide'. Apparently, this story became so understandably
embedded in the Jewish consciousness, that the writer
comments: 'As it is said to this day, "On the mount of the
Lord it shall be provided"' (Gen. 22:14).

A literal translation of this Jewish proverb is: 'On the
mountain of the Lord it will become clear.' In other words,
it is when we get to the point where we are prepared in our
hearts to sacrifice what is nearest and dearest to us – only
then do things become clear. While we are still holding
back parts of our lives or people in our lives or our
possessions or our strengths, very little is clear. We are
confused and the Lord does not seem to provide.

Time after time this is demonstrated when I discuss with
people the theme of God's guidance, whether for myself or
for others. God seems deliberately to withhold clarity and
certainty from us so that he can deal with unsurrendered
areas of our lives. I was listening recently to a woman from
Haiti who runs an orphanage for over sixty children in
Port-au-Prince. Several years ago she was studying in the
United States, debating whether to return with her

husband to Haiti. There was no clear guidance until she was prepared to relinquish her lifestyle in America. When she did return, she joined the board of this orphanage, at a time when they were searching unsuccessfully for a new director. There was complete uncertainty about the person God wanted until she was prepared to put her very considerable gifts at the Lord's disposal for this work – her love for children, her nursing training and experience, her administrative ability, and her home and husband; i.e. her strengths and the people and gifts she prized most.

UNQUESTIONED LOYALTY

When Abraham had come through this gruelling test, God was able to say, 'Now I know that you fear God, seeing that you have not withheld your son, your only son, from me'(Gen. 22:12). The logical part of us wants to say, 'Why did God have to go to that extent to prove what he must have already known?' But, again, such thoughts seem to miss the point of the way God deepens our friendship with him. He longs to bring us to the place where we trust him with all that we hold most precious, and where our loyalty to him is unquestioned. The more we come through that kind of testing circumstance, the more he can entrust us with all that he wants our lives to be.

It is in such light that we must briefly address an objection frequently raised against the entire morality of this story. How, it is often argued, could God possibly countenance even the possibility of human sacrifice? Is this not a classic case of the end justifying the means – anything is allowed, if it produces the right results? Pausing to remember that human sacrifice was widely practised in the Middle East in Abraham's time, we can appreciate the incisive wisdom of Marcus Dods' comment:

So far from introducing into Abraham's mind erroneous ideas about sacrifice, this incident finally dispelled from his mind such ideas, and permanently fixed in his mind the conviction that the sacrifice God seeks is the devotion of a living soul, not the consumption of a dead body (Marcus Dods, op.cit., p.200).

God's answer to Abraham's obedience is, not simply to repeat his promise of blessing reaching out through his descendants to every nation on the face of the earth, but to make the promise even more solemn and sure by an oath: 'By myself I have sworn, says the Lord... I will indeed bless you, and I will multiply your descendants' (Gen. 22:16–18). A promise, a covenant, an oath: what more could God say? In every situation in Abraham's life, God moved to initiate faith. To each act of obedient faith, God responded with another gracious self-disclosure. So Abraham was able to push back the frontiers of living by faith, in a friendship which Jesus invites us to share:

You are my friends, if you do what I command you.... No longer do I call you servants, for the servant does not know what his master is doing; but I have called you friends, for all that I have heard from my Father I have made known to you (John 15:14,15).

The fundamental seriousness of such obedience in our friendship with the Lord is uniquely stressed by James:

Do you want to be shown, you shallow man, that faith apart from works is barren? Was not Abraham our father justified by works, when he offered Isaac upon the altar? You see that faith was active along with his works, and faith was completed by works, and the scripture was fulfilled which says, 'Abraham believed God, and it was reckoned to him as righteousness'; and he was called the friend of God (James 2:20–3).

12   KEEPING A PERSPECTIVE

When we have opted into living by faith in response to the Lord's call, it is very difficult to combine a proper sense of urgency with a calm sense of perspective. We do not want to throw away the unique opportunities of each day or the unrepeatable potential of our one life. We want to fulfil as completely as possible our vocation in the Lord. But if we press ourselves, and those close to us, too hard in our zeal to make our one life count for God, we can easily lose, not just our poise and peace, but any sense of perspective about the way our contribution fits in to the wider purposes of God – both in terms of the past and of the future. We speak and behave as though God had not been in operation until we came on the scene, as though our little part of the world today is centre-stage for God's present activity, and as though God has to make sure all he wants to do in the world is successfully completed before we die.

One of the simplest examples of this lack of perspective is provided by the extreme parochialism of most Christians. We assume, either with astonishing ignorance or remarkable arrogance (or, conceivably, a bit of both) that our church and our country take first prize in God's merit tables. We talk of the wonderful things God is doing, not in perfectly correct ways which give him the proper credit, but in a self-centred, self-congratulatory and competitive way. American Christians are very prone to this kind of 'centrifugal' thinking – the whole world is reckoned to revolve round what God is doing in the 'good old U.S. of A.' A rediscovered patriotism, not often noticeably distinguished from spiritual renewal, has given this Christian imperialism an unwelcome boost in the new wave of national confidence which has emerged as the post-Vietnam and post-Watergate melancholy has been buried.

SHARING GOD'S VISION

America, however, has no monopoly of parochialism. Very few Christians manage to have a proper, biblical perspective both on God's global operations today and God's eternal purposes throughout and beyond history. One of the strangest facts about the worldwide church today is this: those who have little or no access to the fruits of modern communications are the most acutely sensitive to what God is doing in other parts of the world, almost by some kind of spiritual instinct. There is hardly a single excuse for Christians in western countries not to know what God is doing in other parts of the world: all the information is readily available, if we truly shared God's own missionary concern for his world and his radical vision for his church.

The ignorance amongst Christians in the west about our brothers and sisters in Africa, Latin America and Asia is reprehensible. Recent statistics inform us, for example, that there are more Protestant Christians in Brazil than in any country of the world except the USA; that there are more Christians in China than there are citizens of the United Kingdom; and that probably 17,000 Africans are turning to Christ every day. Our attitude to such demonstrations of God at work do not usually reveal either awareness of their significance, or any proper readiness to be taught by the experiences of Christians elsewhere.

When, by contrast, I have shared with Christians in Uganda or in Chile about God's work in other countries, there has been immediate and maintained interest, costly intercession, and instinctive empathy with Christian brothers and sisters in other countries. I remember being approached at Entebbe airport in Uganda in April 1981 by one of the controllers from the traffic control-tower. He was walking through the passenger area during a short break from duty, when he spotted my clerical collar. He stopped me, warmly shook my hand with both his hands, quizzed me non-stop about the church in Britain, pressed me to exchange names and addresses, and has written to me since that brief encounter. This is not at all unusual in African Christians.

A SENSE OF HISTORY

What has this to do with Abraham and living by faith? As we finish our study of this remarkable man's life, we find ourselves looking at the last years of his walk with God on earth, as recorded in three or four chapters in Genesis (Gen. 23:1-20;24:1-67;25:1-11). It is worth reading these passages right through, because they show a man who had a profound sense of perspective, not just on the present, but on the past and on the future as well. He seems to have been superbly balanced on the knife-edge between the twin dangers of frantic activism and weak passivism. He, like Jesus himself much later, knew where he came from and where he was going (see John 13:3). He had no real clue about the future significance of the promise which God had made to him at the outset: but in the passages now before us he constantly showed a deep appreciation, both of God's wider and more distant purposes, and of their implications for the present time and place.

For example, in a little incident just before these particular chapters, we read this: 'Abraham planted a tamarisk tree in Beersheba' (Gen. 21:33). The fact is recorded apropos of nothing – or so it appears. It follows a dispute with some of Abimelech's servants about a well which had been dug by Abraham in or around Beersheba (Gen. 21:25-32). What is so significant about a well? And why plant a tree once the well has been secured?

My wife was discussing with me recently the way our fairly mobile life has meant we have rarely settled in one home for longer than four or five years. She made this intriguing comment: 'We have never planted a tree anywhere.' Actually, I planted an avocado stone soon after we arrived in Cape Town. A few weeks later my young son ripped the emerging sprout from the ground – which may or may not have been a symbolic act! – but I replaced it carefully. When I went back to that garden over ten years later, I was quite disproportionately delighted to see it grown to eighteen or twenty feet.

But Rosemary's point was significant. You only plant trees if you expect to stay a long time in the place. We have never expected to stay that long. Abraham planted that tamarisk tree in Beersheba, because he reckoned that he – and especially his family – would stay a long time in the land of Canaan. When Abraham planted that tree, he was demonstrating how he was living by faith in God, who had promised the land to him and his descendants for ever. Abraham had a sense of history – past and future. That is why, at the place where he planted the tree, he called specifically on the name of God as 'the Lord, the Everlasting God' (Gen. 21:33). The tamarisk happens also to be an evergreen tree, with a very hard wood and a very long life. Abraham made a good choice.

Abraham planted the tree after ensuring that the well he had dug would not be taken from him. At the time this well was the only piece of ground he could call his own in the land of Canaan; he had no property because the whole territory was in the control of its native tribes. In standing firm for this particular well, Abraham was in faith laying claim to the whole land in accordance with the promise of God. It is, therefore, another example of living by faith in the God of history, past and future. I would not be at all surprised if Abraham planted the tree where he had found the water, both together being a statement of his conviction that God would cause his family to grow and take possession of Canaan.

HE OWNED NOTHING

It is important to stress that Abraham did not possess 'even a foot's length' (Acts 7:5) of the promised land. He did not race around trying to take possession of all that God had promised him. He was content, in faith, to establish one well and plant one tree – as a foretaste of all that was to come in God's own good time. His willingness to wait for that time and not to race ahead of God was crucial to his living by faith. Some Christians today have a habit of wanting everything God has promised now – or sooner, if possible. They seek to pre-empt on earth the life in heaven in all its fullness: and they create unrealistic expectations in their fellow Christians, labelling such anticipation of perfection 'living by faith'. They talk of 'naming and claiming' – urging us to name what God has promised and to claim it by faith . . . with no exceptions, conditions, or postponements allowed. Abraham, the father of all who believe, was content with a well and a tree. He later obtained a cave – as we shall see in a moment. Was his faith small and shallow? I think not.

When Sarah died, nearly forty years after the birth of Isaac (Gen. 23:1–20), Abraham was faced with a quandary: where should he bury her? He owned only a well and a tree in a country whose breadth and length he had traversed for over half a century. But this was the country God had promised to give to his descendants: Sarah had to be buried somewhere in the promised land. Chapter 23 describes in great detail the way Abraham went about purchasing the cave of Machpelah, which lay at the end of a field belonging to a Hittite named Ephron. This was located at Hebron, or Mamre, where Abraham had lived in the early days (Gen. 13:18). Following strict commercial practice, Abraham obtained 'the field with the cave that was in it and all the trees that were in the field' (Gen. 23:17).

Living for a while in New England, I can appreciate the significance of Abraham's choice of a burial-place for his family far better than when I lived in the towns and cities of England. Comparatively few people today are buried –

if they are buried, not cremated – in a place which carried great significance for the family. Vermont, however, is riddled with cemeteries. The village where we are living might have five hundred inhabitants, I suppose – but I have already seen four cemeteries within a very small radius, without looking for them; there may be others. The reason, I am told, is that people want to be buried where their family roots are, where they feel they belong. It is a deep-seated and long-established practice, not just in New England but in many parts of the world.

FUTURE GENERATIONS

The cave of Machpelah became highly significant and symbolic in later generations. As we might expect, Abraham himself was buried there, nearly forty years after his wife's death (Gen. 25:9,10). So also was Isaac (Gen. 35:27–9). So, finally, was Jacob, which meant a lengthy, costly and immensely moving trek from Egypt, attended by Joseph and all the pomp and circumstance of Egyptian funeral ceremonies (Gen. 50:1–14). Abraham, Isaac and Jacob; Sarah, Rebekah and Leah: all were buried in the cave of Machpelah. Each burial was an act of faith, showing a sharp awareness of the past and the future as under the sovereign control of the Lord God. It is not surprising to find him constantly revealing himself to later generations as the God of Abraham, Isaac and Jacob.

Indeed, this continuing conviction about God's promised land assumed even more impressive shape in the dying words of Jacob's son, Joseph. After his remarkable career as Pharaoh's number two in Egypt, we might have expected him to be buried there. But, 'Joseph said to his brothers, "I am about to die; but God will visit you, and bring you up out of this land to the land which he swore to give to Abraham, Isaac and Jacob." Then Joseph took an oath of the sons of Israel, saying, "God will visit you, and you shall carry up my bones from here." So Joseph died, being a hundred and ten years old; and they embalmed him, and he was put in a coffin in Egypt' (Gen. 50:24–6).

And there it would have ended. We would, quite reasonably, have concluded that Joseph was overwhelmed, in his dying moments, by an understandable nostalgia for his roots. But we would then be overlooking Joseph's words: 'God will visit you, and bring you up out of this land to the land he swore to Abraham, Isaac and Jacob.' The promise of such a rescue operation had been made by God to Abraham during that deep sleep which came upon him at twilight, immediately before God made a covenant with him. He had been told then that his descendants would be oppressed as slaves in a foreign land for 400 years (Gen. 15:13).

Joseph was basing his prediction on that word from the Lord to his great-grandfather. Four hundred years later, as Moses led the children of Israel out of life-long bondage in Egypt – with plenty of other things to occupy his mind as they had to leave with such haste – he 'took the bones of Joseph with him' (Ex. 13:19). It was probably another hundred years before those bones were buried in the promised land: the facts are recorded at the end of the book of Joshua (Jos. 24:32). So there were five hundred years between Joseph's statement and its fulfilment: faith brings perspective, because it has a sense of history.

I cannot resist one further detail in the story of Abraham's burial. We read this startling sentence: 'Isaac and Ishmael his sons buried him in the cave of Machpelah' (Gen. 25:9). I had never seen this in the Bible until today. I find it deeply moving. Abraham never expected to see Ishmael again, after he was told by God to send him away, some time after the birth of Isaac. We do not know if Abraham did see Ishmael before he died; but Ishmael, whose attitude to his family had been summed up as being 'over against all his kinsmen' (Gen. 16:12;cf.25:18), was alongside Isaac at their father's graveside, now a man of ninety. A father's death can achieve much to reconcile children who have been irretrievably alienated during his

lifetime. But whatever the truth about Ishmael's re-
appearance at his father's funeral, it speaks to me of the
way God is always in sovereign control of a family's
development. Living by faith is always full of surprises
because God loves to surprise us with totally unexpected
blessings. Ishmael's presence at the graveside is, for me,
one of those extra-special bonuses so typical of friendship
with Almighty God.

FINDING THE RIGHT WIFE

There is one final story in the Genesis account of
Abraham's life – the discovery of a wife for his son, Isaac
(Gen. 24:1–67). The way Abraham proceeds with this
amply illustrates his sense of history. There were two
determinative criteria in finding the right woman – she
had to come from Abraham's own country and kindred in
Mesopotamia; but Isaac must not return to Mesopotamia
to live. These two considerations were uppermost in
Abraham's mind because of God's promise to him about
his descendants and the land of Canaan. He reckoned that
the two must never be separated. He was looking back to
what God had told him in the past, and he was looking
ahead to what God had told him about the future.

Abraham's freedom to trust the Lord to provide a wife
for Isaac in such circumstances gives us an example of
living by faith, which is arguably more striking and
instructive than any other part of his life. Let us pause to
list the obstacles to his faith. He was too old to do anything
about it himself; he had to stay at home because a
thousand-mile journey was simply not possible – even if
he had wanted to go. He had, therefore, to entrust the
whole mission to 'his servant, the oldest of his house, who
had charge of all that he had' (Gen. 24:2). This man was
sent off to a country which he had, almost certainly, never
seen (it seems likely that his name was Eliezer of
Damascus, whom Abraham had mentioned as his likely

heir if no son was forthcoming – (Gen. 15:2). Moreover, Abraham himself had not been back to Mesopotamia in over seventy-five years.

Abraham did, however, know some details about the family of his brother, Nahor, who had remained in Mesopotamia. He had been told that Nahor and Milcah, his wife, had eight sons (Gen. 22:20-3). Since he and Sarah had waited such an interminably long time for just one son, there was every chance that all or most of Nahor's sons would have married long ago and had children of their own. The mission of Eliezer to Mesopotamia was not uninformed with practical common sense.

But it required immense faith to carry it through. Anything might have happened to Eliezer, who was no youngster himself. The servant, however loyal and trustworthy, could have lost his nerve at the crucial moment. As Eliezer himself warned, he might find the right woman, but she might not see things the same way (Gen. 24:5) – it has been known to happen!

TAKING RISKS

Abraham was, therefore, taking risks in the whole venture; but living by faith involves risk-taking. The greatest risk of all was that the entire mission might fail: Abraham himself acknowledged this, when he told his servant that he would be absolved from his oath, if the woman would not accompany him back to Canaan (Gen. 24:8). Many things are missed because Abraham's spiritual descendants often find it very hard to take risks, and in particular to face failure. Abraham's friendship with the Lord gave him the security to be unafraid of failure: to be a friend of God was far more important than to succeed in God's service.

Living by faith also involves taking the risk of trusting others with our most cherished and valuable concerns. Abraham knew his senior servant as well as anyone. He had taught him the friendship of the Lord. He had shared with him the priorities of faith. He had in his own lifestyle exemplified trust and obedience, in the midst of many doubts and fears. At the right time he could, with confidence, entrust this sensitive and vital responsibility to the man. The whole narrative illustrates the way the servant had mastered the secret of living by faith in God – 'the God of my master Abraham' (Gen. 24:12,27) indeed, but also the Lord whom he himself had come to worship as his own friend and guide: 'As for me, the Lord has led me in the way . . .' (Gen. 24:12,26,27,52).

Eliezer – if that was his name – would never have grown in his own friendship with the Lord if Abraham had not been free to give him this new dimension of responsibility. We often deny our very claim to be ministers of the Gospel by the way we refuse to trust others with work which really stretches their faith. Many Christians have stopped growing in their friendship with the Lord, have virtually ceased living by faith, because those who pastor them behave like frightened babysitters, not trusting parents. Christians are not babies in a creche, but pilgrims on a journey.

Abraham is described as a pilgrim throughout these chapters in Genesis, and particularly in one important passage in the New Testament (Heb. 11:10–16). His pilgrimage was not nomadic, with no sense of history or destination. He knew where he came from; he knew where he was going – however imprecise his appreciation of its detailed fulfilment. He was completely content to do what God wanted him to do, and to let God fit that life of faithfulness into his wider and greater purposes. His determination to find a wife for Isaac in Mesopotamia had nothing to do with nostalgia: as the writer to the Hebrews expressly states, 'If they had been thinking of that land from which they had gone out, they would have had opportunity to return' (Heb. 11:15). If Abraham had been fired with any longing to return to his roots, he would have done so long before.

LOOKING FORWARD

No, Abraham looked forward – not just to a literal fulfilment of God's promise in a son, a land, a huge family, and much material blessing. 'He looked forward to the city which has foundations, whose builder and maker is God' (Heb. 11:10). His whole lifestyle demonstrated that he was …'seeking a homeland' (Heb. 11:14), that he desired 'a better country, that is, a heavenly one' (Heb. 11:16). However vaguely, Abraham had seen that city, that homeland, that country, with the eyes of faith. He had 'greeted it from afar' (Heb. 11:13). Because he had seen it and by faith made it his own, he knew he could never settle contentedly anywhere on earth. Physical and material possessions became unimportant as compared with this eternal inheritance.

Living by faith is, therefore, necessarily bound up with a rich appreciation of God's eternal purposes. We grow in that faith as we see all that God has done over the centuries with the spiritual descendants of Abraham. We do not hark back nostalgically to the days of Abraham or the life of the early church; instead, we have a lively and constructive approach to church history from Abraham through the apostles to today. We do not allow ourselves to become locked away in the narrow confines of our local church or our own land; we look worldwide to learn about and to learn from all that God is doing everywhere. We look forward to the perfect consummation of God's kingdom and the return of Christ in glory, to the time when living by faith is no more, and our friendship with God will be 'face to face' (1 Cor. 13:12).

NOTES

CHAPTER 1

1. Alan Stibbs, *God's Friend*, Inter-Varsity Fellowship, London, 1964, p. 11.
2. Ibid., p. 15.

CHAPTER 5

1. Marcus Dods, *The Book of Genesis* (The Expositor's Bible), Hodder & Stoughton, 1888, p. 141.

CHAPTER 6

1. Stibbs, op. cit., p. 42.
2. Ibid., p. 43.
3. Ibid., p. 43.

CHAPTER 8

1. Dods, op. cit., p. 161.

CHAPTER 11

1. Quoted by Stibbs, op. cit., p. 73.